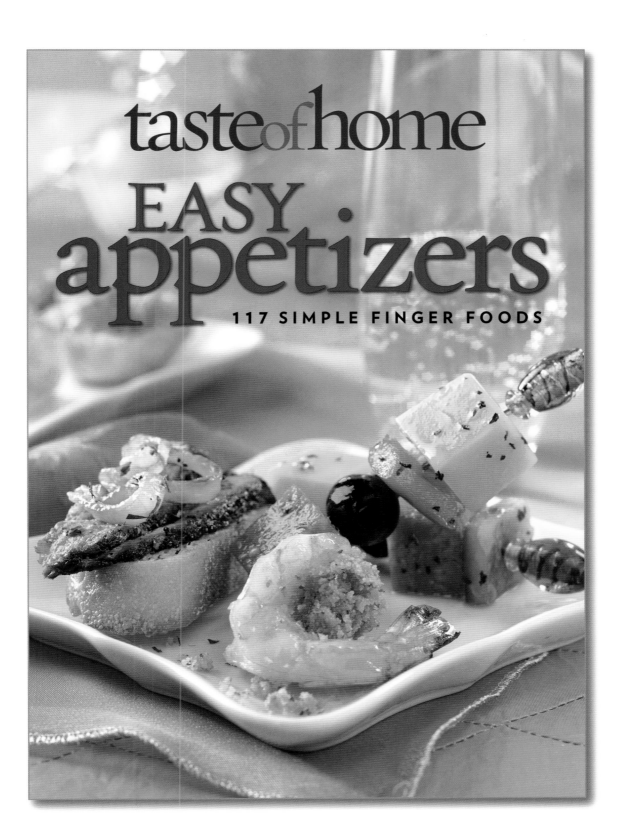

taste of home
EASY
appetizers

117 SIMPLE FINGER FOODS

taste of home

EASY
appetizers

©2009 Reiman Media Group, Inc.
5400 S. 60th St., Greendale WI 53129
All rights reserved.

Senior Vice President, Editor in Chief:	Catherine Cassidy
Vice President, Executive Editor/Books:	Heidi Reuter Lloyd
Creative Director:	Ardyth Cope
Food Director:	Diane Werner RD
Senior Editor/Books:	Mark Hagen
Editor:	Sara Lancaster
Art Director:	Gretchen Trautman
Content Production Supervisor:	Julie Wagner
Layout Designers:	Kathy Crawford, Catherine Fletcher
Proofreader:	Linne Bruskewitz
Recipe Asset Management System:	Coleen Martin, Sue A. Jurack
Premedia Supervisor:	Scott Berger
Recipe Testing and Editing:	Taste of Home Test Kitchen
Food Photography:	Reiman Photo Studio
Editorial Assistant:	Barb Czysz
Cover Photo Photographer:	Rob Hagen
Cover Photo Set Stylist:	Jenny Bradley Vent
Cover Photo Food Stylist:	Sarah Thompson

Chief Marketing Officer:	Lisa Karpinski
Vice President/Book Marketing:	Dan Fink
Creative Director/Creative Marketing:	Jim Palmen

The Reader's Digest Association, Inc.

President and Chief Executive Officer:	Mary G. Berner
President, Food & Entertaining:	Suzanne M. Grimes
President, Consumer Marketing:	Dawn Zier

Pictured on front cover: Pepper-Crusted Tenderloin Crostini (p. 82);
Stuffed Butterflied Shrimp (p. 57); and Antipasto Kabobs (p. 71).
Pictured on back cover: Prosciutto-Wrapped Apricots (p. 55); Turkey Egg Rolls (p. 35);
Cucumber Party Sandwiches (p. 69); and Peanut Butter Mini Muffins (p. 105).

International Standard Book Number (10): 0-89821-754-7
International Standard Book Number (13): 978-0-89821-754-4
Library of Congress Control Number: 2009928536

For other Taste of Home books and products, visit *ShopTasteofHome.com*.

Printed in China.
3 5 7 9 10 8 6 4 2

great gift

Taste of Home Easy Appetizers *makes a great gift for those
who love to nosh or entertain. To order additional copies, specify item number 39328 and send $14.99
(plus $4.99 shipping/processing for one book, $5.99 for two or more) to: Shop Taste of Home, Suite 348,
P.O. Box 26820, Lehigh Valley, PA 18002-6280. To order by credit card, call toll-free 1-800/880-3012.*

Small Bites...
Big Flavor!

If food makes or breaks a party, make sure your celebration includes the "A-list" hors d'oeuvres inside *Taste of Home Easy Appetizers*. This sumptuous array of starters makes it easier than ever to create a palate-pleasing buffet of dips, spreads, canapes, crostini, pinwheels—even beverages and bite-sized desserts!

From simple snacks to chic treats, *Taste of Home Easy Appetizers* removes the fuss but leaves the "wow." With an assortment of 117 easy-to-make, fun-to-eat finger foods and beverages, you'll be creating excuses to host an event.

Looking for some game-day fare? Grab a handful of Pesto Chili Peanuts (p. 22), then fill your plate with Hearty Poppers (p. 51), Honey Garlic Ribs (p. 54) and Baked Chicken Nachos (p. 50).

Are upscale nibbles more appropriate? Impress guests with pretty Asian Spring Rolls (p. 39), unique Prosciutto-Wrapped Apricots (p. 55) and stunning Stuffed Butterflied Shrimp (p. 57).

And don't neglect desserts and beverages. Cream-Filled Strawberries (p. 107), Lemon Tea Cakes (p. 103), Frosty Mocha Drink (p. 96), Champagne Party Punch (p. 96) and a host of other decadent delights lend a sweet ending to your affair.

Eight enticing chapters—Dips & Spreads; Mixes & Munchies; Wrapped & Rolled; Hot & Hearty; Cool & Tasty; Grab & Go; Coffee & Beverages and Sweet & Decadent—hold the key to a memorable gathering.

With common ingredients, clear instructions, clever tips and full-color photos, *Taste of Home Easy Appetizers* serves up irresistible party fare you'll savor down to the last frilled toothpick.

contents

fluffy fruit dip, p. 11

Cool, flavorful dips, thick, chunky salsas and smooth, creamy spreads create some of the most tongue-tingling sidekicks for your favorite snacks.

dips&spreads

CLASSIC SPINACH DIP
PREP: 10 MIN. + CHILLING YIELD: 1-1/2 CUPS

JOYCE FOGLEMAN STAFFORD, TX

Everywhere I take this rich, creamy dip, I'm asked for the recipe. Because it's so delectable, I don't make it at home. I'm afraid that's all I'd eat throughout the day.

4 cups fresh baby spinach, chopped

2 tablespoons water

2/3 cup sliced water chestnuts, chopped

1/3 cup sour cream

1/3 cup mayonnaise

4 teaspoons vegetable soup mix

1 green onion, chopped

Assorted crackers

> In a microwave-safe bowl, combine spinach and water. Cover and microwave on high for 45-60 seconds or until wilted; drain. Cool slightly and squeeze dry.

> In a small bowl, combine the water chestnuts, sour cream, mayonnaise, soup mix, onion and spinach. Chill for at least 1 hour. Serve with crackers.

Editor's Note: This recipe was tested in a 1,100-watt microwave.

CHUNKY BLOODY MARY SALSA
PREP/TOTAL TIME: 15 MIN. YIELD: 1-1/2 CUPS

JESSIE APFEL BERKELEY, CA

Lemon and lime juices lend a citrus tang to this simple salsa, while horseradish gives it a slight kick. It's a wonderful change of pace from the usual store-bought variety.

1 teaspoon prepared horseradish

1 teaspoon lemon juice

1/2 teaspoon lime juice

1/2 teaspoon Worcestershire sauce

2 to 3 drops hot pepper sauce

2 medium tomatoes, seeded and chopped

9 green onions, chopped

1/4 teaspoon salt

Tortilla chips

> In a small bowl, combine the first five ingredients. Stir in the tomatoes, onions and salt. Refrigerate until serving.

> Transfer to a serving bowl with a slotted spoon; serve with tortilla chips.

PAULA MARCHESI
LENHARTSVILLE, PA

It seems I'm always making this zesty salsa packed with peanuts and fruit. I've passed on the recipe too many times to count.

ROASTED PEANUT SALSA

PREP: 15 MIN. + CHILLING YIELD: 4 CUPS

3 tablespoons lime juice

2 tablespoons minced fresh parsley

1 tablespoon canola oil

2-1/2 teaspoons brown sugar

1 to 2 garlic cloves, minced

1/2 to 1 teaspoon crushed red pepper flakes

1/4 teaspoon salt

3/4 cup diced peeled jicama

3/4 cup diced unpeeled apple

1/2 cup chopped cucumber

1/2 cup chopped sweet red pepper

1/2 cup fresh dark sweet cherries, pitted and quartered, optional

3 green onions, sliced

1 cup unsalted dry roasted peanuts

Assorted crackers

> In a large bowl, combine the first seven ingredients. Add the jicama, apple, cucumber, red pepper, cherries if desired and green onions; toss to coat.

> Cover and refrigerate for at least 2 hours. Just before serving, stir in peanuts. Serve with crackers.

tips&ideas

Roasted Peanut Salsa is a delicious way to try a new ingredient, jicama. Jicama (HEE-kah-mah) is a root vegetable resembling a turnip that is also known as a Mexican potato. It has thin brown skin, white flesh, crunchy texture and a sweet, nutty flavor. Look for firm, heavy jicamas with unblemished skin. Store whole jicamas in the refrigerator for up to 3 weeks. Wash, dry and peel before using.

MARY SPENCER
WAUKESHA, WI

This creamy dip is a family favorite. My sister, Teresa, got this recipe from a friend and she passed it along to me. It's loaded with cheese, artichokes and just the right amount of spice.

CREAMY ARTICHOKE DIP

PREP: 20 MIN. COOK: 1 HOUR YIELD: 5 CUPS

2 cans (14 ounces each) water-packed artichoke hearts, rinsed, drained and coarsely chopped

2 cups (8 ounces) shredded part-skim mozzarella cheese

1 package (8 ounces) cream cheese, cubed

1 cup shredded Parmesan cheese

1/2 cup mayonnaise

1/2 cup shredded Swiss cheese

2 tablespoons lemon juice

2 tablespoons plain yogurt

1 tablespoon seasoned salt

1 tablespoon chopped seeded jalapeno pepper

1 teaspoon garlic powder

Tortilla chips

> In a 3-qt. slow cooker, combine the first 11 ingredients. Cover and cook on low for 1 hour or until mixture is heated through. Serve with tortilla chips.

Editor's Note: When cutting hot peppers, disposable gloves are recommended. Avoid touching your face.

tips&ideas

If you have to cut a large number of jalapeno peppers for various recipes, try this time-saving tip. First cut off the tops of the peppers, then slice them in half the long way. Use the small end of a melon baller to easily scrape out the seeds and membranes. It speeds the job along and keeps you from accidentally slicing your gloves.

FRUIT AND CARAMEL BRIE
PREP/TOTAL TIME: 15 MIN. YIELD: 8 SERVINGS

TRACY SCHUHMACHER PENFIELD, NY
I'm a stay-at-home mom who enjoys cooking—especially when I have a new appetizer recipe to try. Brie is one of my favorite cheeses, so this sweet-savory combo is one I love to make.

1 round (8 ounces) Brie cheese, rind removed

1/3 cup caramel ice cream topping

1/4 cup dried cranberries

1/4 cup chopped dried apples

1/4 cup chopped walnuts

1 loaf (1 pound) French bread baguette, sliced and toasted

> Place Brie in a microwave-safe bowl. In a small bowl, combine the caramel topping, cranberries, apples and walnuts. Spread over Brie. Microwave, uncovered, on high for 60-90 seconds or until cheese is heated through and slightly melted. Serve with toasted baguette slices.

Editor's Note: This recipe was tested in a 1,100-watt microwave.

TORTELLINI WITH ROASTED RED PEPPER DIP
PREP/TOTAL TIME: 25 MIN. YIELD: 10 SERVINGS

MICHELLE BOUCHER MILFORD, NH
This unique, warm treat is sure to be a hit with any hungry crowd! Using green spinach tortellini adds a dash of festive color to the serving platter.

1 package (19 ounces) frozen cheese tortellini

1 jar (7 ounces) roasted sweet red peppers, drained

3 garlic cloves, minced

1/2 cup fat-free mayonnaise

1/2 teaspoon balsamic vinegar

1/4 teaspoon salt

1/8 teaspoon pepper

1 tablespoon olive oil

1 large zucchini, cut into strips

> Prepare tortellini according to package directions. Meanwhile, place red peppers and garlic in a food processor; cover and process until combined. Add the mayonnaise, vinegar, salt and pepper; cover and process until blended. Transfer to a small bowl.

> Drain tortellini; toss with oil. Serve with zucchini strips and red pepper dip.

FRUIT SALSA WITH CINNAMON CHIPS

PREP/TOTAL TIME: 30 MIN. YIELD: 2-1/2 CUPS SALSA (80 CHIPS)

JESSICA ROBINSON INDIAN TRAIL, NC
I first made this fresh, fruity salsa for a family baby shower. Everyone wanted the recipe. Now, someone makes this juicy snack for just about every family gathering—and I have to keep reminding everyone who introduced it!

1 cup finely chopped fresh strawberries

1 medium navel orange, peeled and finely chopped

3 medium kiwifruit, peeled and finely chopped

1 can (8 ounces) unsweetened crushed pineapple, drained

1 tablespoon lemon juice

1-1/2 teaspoons sugar

CINNAMON CHIPS:

10 flour tortillas (8 inches)

1/4 cup butter, melted

1/3 cup sugar

1 teaspoon ground cinnamon

> In a small bowl, combine the first six ingredients. Cover and refrigerate until serving.

> For chips, brush tortillas with butter; cut each into eight wedges. Combine sugar and cinnamon; sprinkle over tortillas. Place tortillas on ungreased baking sheets.

> Bake at 350° for 5-10 minutes or just until crisp. Serve cinnamon chips with fruit salsa.

PARTY CHEESE BALLS

PREP: 20 MIN. + CHILLING
YIELD: 2 CHEESE BALLS (1-3/4 CUPS EACH)

SHIRLEY HOERMAN NEKOOSA, WI
These tangy cheese balls are guaranteed to spread cheer among guests. The ingredients create a colorful presentation and savory flavor combinaiton. The party-pleasers are also great when you're short on time, as they can be made ahead.

1 package (8 ounces) cream cheese, softened

2 cups (8 ounces) shredded cheddar cheese

1 jar (5 ounces) sharp American cheese spread

1 jar (5 ounces) pimiento cheese spread

3 tablespoons finely chopped onion

1 tablespoon lemon juice

1 teaspoon Worcestershire sauce

Dash garlic salt

1/2 cup chopped pecans, toasted

1/2 cup minced fresh parsley

Assorted crackers

> In a large bowl, beat the first eight ingredients until blended. Cover and refrigerate for 15 minutes or until easy to handle.

> Shape into two balls; roll one ball in pecans and one in parsley. Cover and refrigerate. Remove from the refrigerator 15 minutes before serving with crackers.

SUE PENCE
ALEXANDRIA, VA

We've been making this fruity sensation in my family for generations. Serve it throughout the year with whatever fresh fruits are in season.

FLUFFY FRUIT DIP

PREP: 20 MIN. + CHILLING   YIELD: ABOUT 2-1/2 CUPS

1/2 cup sugar

2 tablespoons all-purpose flour

1 cup unsweetened pineapple juice

1 tablespoon butter

1 egg, lightly beaten

1 cup heavy whipping cream, whipped

Assorted fresh fruit

> In a small saucepan, combine sugar and flour. Gradually whisk in pineapple juice. Add butter. Cook and stir until butter is melted and mixture comes to a boil. Cook and stir for 1-2 minutes or until thickened.

> Remove from the heat. Stir a small amount of hot mixture into egg; return all to the pan, stirring constantly. Bring to a gentle boil; cook and stir for 1 minute. Remove from the heat. Cool to room temperature, stirring several times.

> Fold in whipped cream. Cover and refrigerate for at least 1 hour. Serve with fruit.

Keep perishable dips cold with this handy hint. Fill a large glass or plastic bowl with ice cubes. Then, fill a smaller bowl with the dip and set it on top of the ice. Replace the ice as it melts.

CAROL BARLOW
BERWYN, IL

When my husband and I entertain, we serve this robust spread. The combination of goat cheese, garlic and onions always earns rave reviews.

ROASTED GOAT CHEESE WITH GARLIC

PREP: 45 MIN. BAKE: 15 MIN. YIELD: ABOUT 1-1/4 CUPS

6 to 8 garlic cloves, peeled

1 tablespoon canola oil

1 medium red onion, thinly sliced

2 tablespoons butter

1 tablespoon brown sugar

8 ounces crumbled goat or feta cheese

1 tablespoon white balsamic vinegar

Salt and pepper to taste

1/4 cup thinly sliced fresh basil

Thinly sliced French bread or assorted crackers

> Place garlic and oil in a pie plate. Cover and bake at 350° for 30 minutes.

> Meanwhile, in a small skillet, saute onion in butter until tender and lightly browned. Add brown sugar; cook and stir until sugar is dissolved. Remove from the heat.

> Remove garlic from pie plate. Spread onion mixture in pie plate; top with cheese. Place garlic over cheese. Bake, uncovered, for 15-20 minutes or until cheese is melted.

> Mash garlic mixture with a fork. Stir in the vinegar, salt and pepper. Transfer to a serving bowl; sprinkle with basil. Serve warm with French bread or assorted crackers.

HOT & SPICY CRANBERRY DIP

PREP/TOTAL TIME: 15 MIN. YIELD: 2 CUPS

DOROTHY PRITCHETT WILLS POINT, TX
This deliciously different dip packs in plenty of zip. The cranberry flavor is wonderful with mini sausage links.

1 can (16 ounces) jellied cranberry sauce

2 to 3 tablespoons prepared horseradish

2 tablespoons honey

1 tablespoon Worcestershire sauce

1 tablespoon lemon juice

1 garlic clove, minced

1/4 to 1/2 teaspoon ground cayenne pepper

Pineapple chunks

Orange sections

Mini precooked sausages, warmed

> In a medium saucepan, combine first seven ingredients. Bring to a boil. Reduce heat and simmer, covered, 5 minutes. Serve warm with pineapple, oranges and sausages.

EGGNOG DIP

PREP: 10 MIN. + CHILLING COOK: 10 MIN. + COOLING
YIELD: ABOUT 2-1/2 CUPS

SHARON MACDONNELL LANTZVILLE, BC
I put together a cookbook of my grandma's Christmas recipes that includes this classic eggnog appetizer. Serve it as a dip with fresh fruit or drizzle it over cake for dessert.

1-1/2 cups eggnog

2 tablespoons cornstarch

1/2 cup sour cream

1/2 cup heavy whipping cream

1 tablespoon sugar

1/2 teaspoon rum extract, optional

Assorted fruit and pound cake cubes

> In a small saucepan, combine the eggnog and cornstarch until smooth. Bring to a boil; boil and stir for 2 minutes. Remove from the heat; stir in sour cream. Cool completely.

> In a small bowl, beat whipping cream and sugar until stiff peaks form. Fold into eggnog mixture with extract if desired. Cover and refrigerate overnight. Serve with fruit and cake cubes.

Editor's Note: This recipe was tested with commercially prepared eggnog.

BAKED ASPARAGUS DIP

PREP/TOTAL TIME: 30 MIN. YIELD: ABOUT 2 CUPS

SANDRA BARATKA PHILLIPS, WI
Because I'm from Wisconsin, I thought it was appropriate to create a recipe that featured a vegetable and a cheese—two of the things my state produces in abundance.

1 pound diced cooked fresh asparagus, drained

1 cup grated Parmesan cheese

1 cup mayonnaise

Snack rye bread

> In a large bowl, combine the asparagus, cheese and mayonnaise. Place in a 2-cup ovenproof bowl. Bake at 375° for 20 minutes or until heated through. Serve with bread.

LAYERED ASIAN DIP

PREP: 20 MIN. YIELD: 10 SERVINGS

BONNIE MAZUR REEDSBURG, WI

Guests are quick to dig into this irresistible dip. With tender chunks of chicken and lots of Asian seasoning, it's a tasty switch from the usual taco flavor variety.

1 cup chopped cooked chicken breast

1/2 cup shredded carrot

1/4 cup chopped unsalted peanuts

3 tablespoons chopped green onions

3 tablespoons reduced-sodium soy sauce, divided

1 tablespoon minced fresh parsley

1 garlic clove, minced

1 teaspoon sesame seeds, toasted

2 tablespoons packed brown sugar

1-1/2 teaspoons cornstarch

1/2 cup water

2 tablespoons ketchup

1-1/2 teaspoons Worcestershire sauce

1/2 teaspoon cider vinegar

2 drops hot pepper sauce

1 package (8 ounces) reduced-fat cream cheese

Tortilla chips

> In a large bowl, combine the chicken, carrot, peanuts, onions, 2 tablespoons soy sauce, parsley, garlic and sesame seeds. Cover and refrigerate for several hours.

> In a large saucepan, combine the brown sugar and cornstarch; stir in water, ketchup, Worcestershire sauce, vinegar and hot pepper sauce until smooth. Bring to a boil; cook and stir for 1-2 minutes or until thickened. Cool for 5 minutes. Cover sauce and refrigerate.

> Just before serving, in a small bowl, beat cream cheese and remaining soy sauce until smooth. Spread evenly into a 12-in. serving dish. Cover with chicken mixture; drizzle with sauce. Serve with tortilla chips.

SPRUCED-UP CHEESE SPREAD

PREP/TOTAL TIME: 20 MIN. YIELD: 4 CUPS

JUDY GRIMES BRANDON, MS

My neighbor gave me the recipe for this zippy, cheesy cracker spread. During the holidays, it's easy to shape the spread into a Christmas tree shape for a festive presentation.

1 jar (4 ounces) diced pimientos, drained, divided

1 small onion, grated

1 cup mayonnaise

1 to 2 tablespoons prepared mustard

1 tablespoon Worcestershire sauce

1 teaspoon celery seed

1/2 teaspoon paprika

1/4 teaspoon garlic salt

3 cups (12 ounces) finely shredded sharp cheddar cheese

2 tablespoons finely chopped pecans

Minced fresh parsley

Assorted crackers

> Set aside 2 tablespoons pimientos for topping. In a large bowl, combine the remaining pimientos and the next seven ingredients. Stir in cheese.

> Transfer to a serving bowl; sprinkle with pecans, parsley and reserved pimientos. Serve spread with assorted crackers.

EDNA HOFFMAN
HEBRON, IN

Delight guests with this decadent, non-traditional fondue. Creamy apple butter and cinnamon red hots add tangy, tongue-tingling flair!

RASPBERRY FONDUE DIP

PREP/TOTAL TIME: 25 MIN. YIELD: 1 CUP

1 package (10 ounces) frozen sweetened raspberries

1 cup apple butter

1 tablespoon red-hot candies

2 teaspoons cornstarch

Assorted fresh fruit

> Place raspberries in a small bowl; set aside to thaw. Strain raspberries, reserving 1 tablespoon juice; discard seeds.

> In a small saucepan, combine the strained berries, apple butter and red-hots; cook over medium heat until candies are dissolved, stirring occasionally.

> In a small bowl, combine cornstarch and reserved juice until smooth; stir into berry mixture. Bring to a boil; cook and stir over medium heat for 1-2 minutes or until thickened.

> Transfer to a serving dish, fondue pot or 1-1/2-qt. slow cooker. Serve warm or cold with assorted fresh fruit.

CAROLYN DEKRYGER
FREMONT, MI

I always come home with an empty plate when I take this special appetizer to parties. While the cheesy, pleasing starter looks fancy, it is actually quite easy to make.

BAKED BRIE

PREP: 15 MIN. + CHILLING BAKE: 15 MIN. + STANDING YIELD: 8 SERVINGS

1/4 cup butter, softened

1 package (3 ounces) cream cheese softened

3/4 cup all-purpose flour

1 round (8 ounces) Brie or Camembert cheese

1 egg

1 teaspoon water

Assorted crackers and fresh fruit

> In a large bowl, beat the butter, cream cheese and flour on low speed until mixture forms a ball. Divide in half and wrap each portion in plastic wrap; refrigerate for 30 minutes.

> On a lightly floured surface, roll out each portion into a 7-in. circle about 1/8 in. thick. Place one circle on an ungreased baking sheet. Place Brie on pastry and top with remaining pastry circle; pinch edges to seal. Flute bottom edge if desired.

> In a small bowl, whisk egg and water; brush over top and sides of pastry. Bake at 400° for 15-20 minutes or until golden brown. Immediately remove from the baking sheets. Let stand for 30 minutes before serving. Serve with crackers and fruit.

tips&ideas

Brie and Camembert cheese fall under the category of soft-ripened cheeses. Feta and goat cheese are additional varieties listed in this category. These are cheeses ripened with bacteria, and may have a creamy—and sometimes spreadable—consistency.

CRAN-APPLE SALSA

PREP/TOTAL TIME: 15 MIN. YIELD: 5 CUPS

JODY BAUER BALATON, MN

Here's a festive twist on traditional holiday cranberry relish. This salsa packs in a tart-sweet blend of fresh flavors, goes together in minutes and looks stunning. We think it makes the perfect party dip to celebrate the season.

1 package (12 ounces) fresh or frozen cranberries, thawed

3 medium apples, cut into wedges

1 medium sweet red pepper, cut into pieces

1 small red onion, chopped

1/2 cup sugar

1/3 cup unsweetened apple juice

3 tablespoons minced fresh cilantro

2 tablespoons chopped jalapeno pepper

1 teaspoon grated lime peel

Tortilla chips

> In a food processor, process the cranberries, apples, red pepper and onion in batches until coarsely pureed.

> Transfer to a serving bowl. Stir in the sugar, apple juice, cilantro, jalapeno and lime peel. Refrigerate until serving. Serve with tortilla chips.

Editor's Note: When cutting hot peppers, disposable gloves are recommended. Avoid touching your face.

REUBEN SPREAD

PREP: 5 MIN. COOK: 3 HOURS YIELD: ABOUT 5 CUPS

PAM ROHR TROY, OH

You'll need only five ingredients to stir up this simple, hearty snack that tastes like a Reuben sandwich. I'm requested to bring it to all the gatherings I attend.

2-1/2 cups cubed cooked corned beef

1 jar (16 ounces) sauerkraut, rinsed and well drained

2 cups (8 ounces) shredded Swiss cheese

2 cups (8 ounces) shredded cheddar cheese

1 cup mayonnaise

Snack rye bread

> In a 3-qt. slow cooker, combine the first five ingredients. Cover and cook on low for 3 hours, stirring occasionally. Serve warm with rye bread.

tips&ideas

For an appetizer buffet that serves as the meal, offer five or six different options (including some substantial selections) and plan on eight to nine pieces per guest. If you will be serving a meal in addition to the appetizers, plan on two to three pieces per person.

curried pecans, p. 25

Liven up your party by setting out a bowl filled with these snackable mixes and munchies. Just one handful will bring you back to nibble some more.

munchies&mixes

CINDY WINTER-HARLEY
CARY, NC

Satisfy a midday snack-attack with these terrific cheesy pretzels. The coated rods get great flavor from garlic powder, oregano and spicy cayenne.

PARMESAN PRETZEL RODS

PREP: 10 MIN. BAKE: 20 MIN. + COOLING YIELD: ABOUT 2-1/2 DOZEN

1 cup grated Parmesan cheese

1 teaspoon garlic powder

1 teaspoon dried oregano

1/2 teaspoon cayenne pepper

6 tablespoons butter, cubed

1/4 cup olive oil

1 package (10 ounces) pretzel rods

> In a small bowl, combine the Parmesan cheese, garlic powder, oregano and cayenne; set aside. In a small saucepan, heat butter and oil until butter is melted. Coat two-thirds of each pretzel rod with butter mixture, then roll in cheese mixture. Reheat butter mixture if needed.

> Place in an ungreased 15-in. x 10-in. baking pan. Bake at 275° for 20-25 minutes or until golden brown, turning once. Cool. Store in an airtight container.

tips&ideas

For those with a sweet tooth, whip up a batch of Cinnamon-Sugar Pretzel Rods. For cinnamon-sugar pretzels, omit the Parmesan cheese, garlic powder, oregano and cayenne, and stir 2 tablespoons honey into the butter and olive oil mixture instead. Coat the pretzel rods with the butter mixture, then sprinkle with a mixture of 1/2 cup granulated sugar and 1 teaspoon ground cinnamon.

HOLIDAY ALMONDS

PREP/TOTAL TIME: 30 MIN. YIELD: 2 CUPS

TRISHA KRUSE EAGLE, ID

These sweet and flavorful nuts are addictive—especially since they are so simple to make. I can have a batch whipped up in half an hour, which comes in handy when I'm expecting company. Plus, I know everyone will love them.

1/2 cup packed brown sugar

1 teaspoon apple pie spice or pumpkin pie spice

1/2 teaspoon curry powder

1/4 teaspoon salt

1 tablespoon egg white

2 cups blanched almonds

> In a small bowl, combine brown sugar and seasonings; set aside. In another bowl, whisk egg white until foamy. Add almonds; toss to coat. Add spice mixture; toss to coat.

> Spread on a greased foil-lined baking sheet. Bake at 325° for 20-25 minutes or until lightly browned, stirring occasionally. Cool completely. Store in an airtight container.

SUGAR 'N' SPICE NUTS

PREP/TOTAL TIME: 30 MIN. YIELD: 3-1/2 CUPS

JOAN KLINEFELTER UTICA, IL

My daughters, grandkids...everyone looks forward to this mouth-watering mix of crunchy nuts, spices and fruit. Tucked in colorful tins, it makes a speedy last-minute gift idea for busy hostesses or drop-in visitors.

1/4 cup packed brown sugar

1/2 teaspoon ground cinnamon

1/4 teaspoon cayenne pepper

1 egg white

1 cup salted cashews

1 cup pecan halves

1 cup dry roasted peanuts

1/2 cup dried cranberries

> In a small bowl, combine the brown sugar, cinnamon and cayenne; set aside. In a large bowl, whisk the egg white; add nuts and cranberries. Sprinkle with sugar mixture and toss to coat. Spread in a single layer on a greased baking sheet.

> Bake at 300° for 18-20 minutes or until golden brown, stirring once. Cool. Store the mix in an airtight container.

ORANGE–CRANBERRY SNACK MIX

PREP: 10 MIN. BAKE: 50 MIN. + COOLING YIELD: 6 CUPS

SARAH GERLACH WILLMAR, MN

With cinnamon, ginger and nutmeg, this sweet mix is perfect for fall. I often make the addictive mix at Thanksgiving.

2 cups each square oat cereal, Corn Chex and miniature pretzels

1/3 cup orange juice concentrate

1/4 cup butter, melted

2 tablespoons brown sugar

1 teaspoon ground cinnamon

3/4 teaspoon ground ginger

1/4 teaspoon ground nutmeg

2/3 cup dried cranberries

> In a large bowl, combine cereals and pretzels. In a small bowl, combine the orange juice concentrate, butter, brown sugar and spices. Pour over cereal mixture; toss to coat. Spread evenly in a foil-lined 15-in. x 10-in. baking pan.

> Bake at 250° for 50 minutes, stirring every 10 minutes. Stir in cranberries. Cool, stirring several times. Store in an airtight container.

PESTO CHILI PEANUTS

PREP/TOTAL TIME: 25 MIN. YIELD: 5 CUPS

DENNIS DAHLIN BOLINGBROOK, IL

Who would ever dream of teaming pesto with peanuts? The result is a can't-stop-eating-'em snack that's salty, savory and sure to be in hot demand with friends and family. Just try it and see how popular it becomes with your gang, too.

1 envelope pesto sauce mix

3 tablespoons olive oil

1 teaspoon chili powder

1/4 teaspoon cayenne pepper

5 cups salted dry roasted peanuts

> In a small bowl, whisk the pesto mix, olive oil, chili powder and cayenne. Pour mixture into a large resealable plastic bag; add peanuts. Seal bag and shake to coat. Transfer to a greased 13-in. x 9-in. baking pan.

> Bake, uncovered, at 350° for 15-20 minutes, stirring once. Spread on waxed paper to cool. Store in an airtight container.

HOT MUSTARD POPCORN

PREP: 10 MIN. YIELD: 3 QUARTS

DIANE HIXON NICEVILLE, FL

When friends pop in, I like to dish up yummy munchies like this popcorn snack. They can't get enough of the zesty flavor combination created by the blend of seasonings.

1 teaspoon ground mustard

1/2 teaspoon dried thyme

1/2 teaspoon salt

1/4 teaspoon pepper

Dash cayenne pepper

3 quarts freshly popped popcorn

> Combine the first five ingredients. Place popcorn in a large bowl; add seasonings and toss to coat. Store in an airtight container.

SUE MURPHY
GREENWOOD, MI

Seasoned with chili powder and cayenne pepper, these paper-thin chips are surefire crowd-pleasers. Add a little more or a little less chili powder and cayenne to adjust the level of spiciness.

FIERY POTATO CHIPS

PREP: 15 MIN. + SOAKING COOK: 5 MIN./BATCH YIELD: 10 CUPS

4 medium unpeeled potatoes

4 teaspoons salt, divided

4 cups ice water

1 tablespoon chili powder

1 teaspoon garlic salt

1 teaspoon dried parsley flakes

1/4 to 1/2 teaspoon cayenne pepper

Oil for frying

> Using a vegetable peeler or metal cheese slicer, cut potatoes into very thin lengthwise strips. Place in a large bowl; add 3 teaspoons salt and ice water. Soak for 30 minutes; drain.

> Place potatoes on paper towels and pat dry. In a small bowl, combine the chili powder, garlic salt, parsley flakes, cayenne and the remaining salt; set seasoning mixture aside.

> In an electric skillet or deep-fat fryer, heat oil to 375°. Cook potatoes in oil in batches for 2-3 minutes or until deep golden brown, stirring the potatoes frequently.

> Remove with a slotted spoon; drain on paper towels. Immediately sprinkle with reserved seasoning mixture. Store in an airtight container.

ABBEY BOYLE
TAMPA, FL

These sassy peanuts are great for football parties, as after-school snacks or movie nights. During the holidays, I'll even prepare them to give as presents.

BARBECUED PEANUTS

PREP: 10 MIN. BAKE: 25 MIN. + COOLING YIELD: 3 CUPS

1/3 cup barbecue sauce

2 tablespoons butter, melted

1 teaspoon garlic powder

1/4 to 1/2 teaspoon cayenne pepper

1 jar (16 ounces) dry roasted peanuts

> In a large bowl, combine the barbecue sauce, butter, garlic powder and cayenne. Add peanuts; stir until evenly coated. Transfer to a greased 13-in. x 9-in. baking pan.

> Bake, uncovered, at 325° for 25-30 minutes, stirring every 10 minutes. Spread on waxed paper; cool completely. Store in an airtight container.

tips&ideas

Hot and spicy, cayenne pepper is made from the cayenne chili. Used both in cooking and medicine, its hot flavor comes from a chemical called capsaicin, which comprises about 12% of the chili. If you don't have cayenne pepper on hand for Barbecued Peanuts, substitute red chili powder, paprika or red pepper flakes.

FLAVORED OYSTER CRACKERS

PREP/TOTAL TIME: 25 MIN. YIELD: 12 CUPS

TASTE OF HOME TEST KITCHEN GREENDALE, WI

These jazzed-up oyster crackers created by our Test Kitchen have such great flavor, we bet you'll have trouble not eating them all at once! With Parmesan cheese and seasoning from a soup mix, they're a surefire hit for snacking or with soup.

2 packages (10 ounces each) oyster crackers

1/2 cup canola oil

1/4 cup grated Parmesan cheese

1 envelope savory herb with garlic soup mix

> Place the crackers in a large bowl. Combine the oil, cheese and soup mix; pour over crackers and toss gently. Transfer to two ungreased 15-in. x 10-in. baking pans.

> Bake at 350° for 5-7 minutes, stirring once. Cool. Store in an airtight container.

tips&ideas

If a recipe calls for grated Parmesan cheese, you can grate your own at home for even more fresh flavor. Simply cut the cheese into 1-inch cubes and process 1 cup of cubes at a time in a food processor on high until finely grated.

CURRIED PECANS

PREP/TOTAL TIME: 30 MIN. YIELD: 2 CUPS

JOYCE SCHULTZ SWIFT CURRENT, SK

These buttery pecans have a mild curry flavor that appeals to all palates. For a real crowd-pleaser, set out a bowl filled with these tempting coated nuts.

3 tablespoons butter, melted

1-1/4 to 1-1/2 teaspoons curry powder

1/2 teaspoon salt

2 cups pecan halves

> In a large bowl, combine the butter, curry powder and salt. Add pecans and toss to coat. Transfer to a foil-lined 11-in. x 7-in. baking pan.

> Bake at 350° for 15-20 minutes or until toasted and crisp, stirring three times. Cool on a wire rack. Store in an airtight container.

SWEET & SPICY SNACK

PREP: 10 MIN. BAKE: 45 MIN. YIELD: 10 CUPS

TASTE OF HOME TEST KITCHEN GREENDALE, WI

Crunchy cereal, cheesy snack crackers and mini pretzels are baked to perfection with a sprinkling of soy sauce, chili powder and barbecue seasoning. The mix is sure to spice up your next party or festive gathering.

4 cups miniature pretzels

2-1/3 cups reduced-fat cheese-flavored baked snack crackers

2 cups Wheat Chex

3 tablespoons butter, melted

1 tablespoon reduced-sodium soy sauce

2 teaspoons chili powder

1 teaspoon barbecue seasoning

3 cups Corn Pops

> In a large bowl, combine the pretzels, crackers and cereal. In a small bowl, combine the butter, soy sauce, chili powder and barbecue seasoning; pour over cereal mixture and toss to evenly coat.

> Transfer mixture to a 15-in. x 10-in. baking pan coated with cooking spray. Bake at 250° for 45 minutes, stirring every 15 minutes. Stir in Corn Pops. Store in airtight containers.

Editor's Note: If barbecue seasoning is not available in your grocery store, try Penzeys Spices. Call 1-800/741-7787 or visit *www.penzeys.com*. Store in an airtight container.

PECANS 'N' CRANBERRIES

PREP: 10 MIN. BAKE: 15 MIN. + COOLING YIELD: ABOUT 4 CUPS

RENE DALRYMPLE HANSVILLE, WA

Spice up a party with this well-seasoned blend of nuts and cranberries—or keep a batch tightly wrapped in the freezer to give as last-minute presents.

2 tablespoons butter, melted

2 tablespoons Worcestershire sauce

1/2 teaspoon ground cumin

1/2 teaspoon garlic powder

1/2 teaspoon seasoned salt

1/4 to 1/2 teaspoon cayenne pepper

3 cups pecan halves

1-1/2 cups dried cranberries

> In a large bowl, combine the first six ingredients. Stir in the pecans. Spread in an ungreased 13-in. x 9-in. baking pan. Bake at 350° for 15 minutes, stirring every 5 minutes. Cool completely. Stir in cranberries. Store in an airtight container.

SHERI WARNER
LOUISVILLE, NE

Looking for something different—and not sweet—for a bake sale? Whip up this fun popcorn snack. It's lightly spiced with pizza seasonings and very munchable.

PIZZA POPCORN

PREP/TOTAL TIME: 20 MIN. YIELD: 2-1/2 QUARTS

2-1/2 quarts popped popcorn

1/3 cup butter, cubed

1/4 cup grated Parmesan cheese

1/2 teaspoon garlic salt

1/2 teaspoon dried oregano

1/2 teaspoon dried basil

1/4 teaspoon salt

1/4 teaspoon onion powder

> Place popcorn in an ungreased 13-in. x 9-in. baking pan. Melt butter in a small saucepan; add the remaining ingredients. Pour over popcorn and mix well. Bake, uncovered, at 350° for 15 minutes.

tips&ideas

Follow these pointers to make perfect popcorn right on the stovetop. Use a 3- or 4-quart pan with a loose-fitting lid to allow the steam to escape. Add 1/3 cup canola oil for every cup of kernels. When the popping begins to slow, remove the pan from the heat—the hot oil will continue to pop the remaining kernels.

JEAN VOAN
SHEPHERD, TX

These seasoned nuts are so good, it's hard to stop eating them. I made them for gift baskets and got many compliments. They are perfect for the holidays but delicious to munch anytime. Package a batch in a festive tin to give as a hostess gift.

SPICY CASHEWS

PREP/TOTAL TIME: 10 MIN. YIELD: 2-2/3 CUPS

2 cans (10 ounces each) salted cashews

3 tablespoons butter

1 tablespoon canola oil

1/2 teaspoon salt

1/2 teaspoon chili powder

1/4 to 1/2 teaspoon crushed red pepper flakes

> In a large skillet, saute cashews in butter and oil for 4-5 minutes or until golden brown. Spread on a paper towel-lined baking sheet; let stand for 2-3 minutes. Transfer to a large bowl. Sprinkle with salt, chili powder and pepper flakes; toss to coat. Store in an airtight container.

tips&ideas

Setting out a large bowl of Spicy Cashews is great for a casual gathering. But for a more upscale affair, create a unique presentation by placing the cashews into foil muffin liners. Arrange a variety of colored liners on a serving tray or simply alternate with gold and silver liners for a stunning look.

PARMESAN PARTY MIX

PREP/TOTAL TIME: 10 MIN. YIELD: 8 CUPS

KAREN SMITH THORNTON, CO

This is our favorite mix. The seasonings add just the right amount of flavor, plus it's a snap to toss together.

7 cups Crispix

2 cups cheese-flavored snack crackers

1 cup pretzel sticks

3 tablespoons olive oil

1 teaspoon Italian seasoning

1/4 teaspoon fennel seed, crushed

1/8 teaspoon hot pepper sauce

1/2 cup grated Parmesan or Romano cheese

> In a 2-gal. resealable plastic bag, combine the cereal, crackers and pretzels. In a small bowl, combine the oil, Italian seasoning, fennel seed and hot pepper sauce.

> Pour over cereal mixture; seal bag and toss to coat. Add Parmesan cheese; seal bag and toss to coat. Store in an airtight container.

tips&ideas

If you don't have Italian seasoning on hand, mix up your own. Substitute 1/4 teaspoon each of basil, thyme, rosemary and oregano for each teaspoon of Italian seasoning called for in a recipe.

BUTTERY TORTILLA SNACK STRIPS

PREP/TOTAL TIME: 20 MIN. YIELD: 1-1/2 DOZEN

KAREN RIORDAN FERN CREEK, KY

These crispy, buttery strips are a flavorful, homemade alternative to ordinary potato chips.

2 tablespoons butter, melted

6 flour tortillas (8 inches)

1/2 teaspoon ground cumin

1/2 teaspoon garlic powder

1/2 teaspoon onion salt or onion powder

Dash to 1/8 teaspoon cayenne pepper, optional

> Brush butter over one side of each tortilla. Combine the seasonings; lightly sprinkle 1/4 teaspoon over each tortilla. Make two stacks of tortillas, with three in each stack. Using a serrated knife, cut each stack into nine thin strips.

> Place in an ungreased 15-in. x 10-in. baking pan. Bake at 400° for 8-10 minutes or until lightly browned. Serve warm.

ranch pizza pinwheels, p. 40

Wrapped, rolled and stuffed with a variety of savory fillings, these scrumptious morsels will delight the palate and please the eyes.

wrapped&rolled

Melt remaining butter; brush over wontons. Coat with croutons. Place on a baking sheet; freeze. Transfer to a large freezer bag; seal and freeze for up to 3 months.

To use frozen wontons: Place wontons on greased baking sheets. Bake at 425° for 10 minutes. Turn; bake 5-10 minutes longer or until lightly browned. Serve warm with sweet-and-sour sauce if desired.

HAM ASPARAGUS SPIRALS

PREP: 20 MIN. BAKE: 15 MIN. YIELD: 20 APPETIZERS

ROSIE HUFFER WESTMINSTER, CA

Just three ingredients are all you will need to prepare these impressive-looking hors d'oeuvres. A vegetable appetizer like this is always a welcomed addition to the table.

20 fresh asparagus spears, trimmed

20 thin slices deli ham

1 package (10.6 ounces) refrigerated Italian breadsticks and garlic spread

> In a large skillet, bring 1/2 in. of water to a boil; add asparagus. Reduce heat; cover and simmer for 2 minutes. Drain and immediately place asparagus in ice water; drain and pat dry.

> Wrap a slice of ham around each asparagus spear. Unroll breadstick dough; spread with garlic spread. Cut each breadstick in half lengthwise. Wrap one piece of dough, garlic spread side out, around each ham-wrapped asparagus spear.

> Place on an ungreased baking sheet. Bake at 375° for 13-15 minutes or until golden brown. Serve the spirals immediately.

CHICKEN WONTON ROLLS

PREP: 40 MIN. + FREEZING BAKE: 15 MIN. YIELD: ABOUT 4 DOZEN

MARY DIXSON DECATUR, AL

Guests will think you fussed over these warm, golden bites. I sometimes turn the recipe into a main course by using egg roll wrappers and serving the rolls with chicken gravy.

1 package (3 ounces) cream cheese, softened

6 tablespoons butter, softened, divided

2 tablespoons minced chives

1/2 teaspoon lemon-pepper seasoning

1-1/2 cups finely chopped cooked chicken

1 can (4 ounces) mushroom stems and pieces, drained and chopped

1 package (12 ounces) wonton wrappers

2/3 cup crushed salad croutons

Sweet-and-sour sauce, optional

> In a small bowl, beat the cream cheese, 2 tablespoons butter, chives and lemon-pepper until blended. Stir in chicken and mushrooms.

> Place a rounded teaspoonful in the center of a wonton wrapper. (Keep remaining wrappers covered with a damp paper towel until ready to use.) Fold bottom corner over filling; fold sides toward center. Moisten remaining corner with water; roll up tightly to seal.

BARBARA KEITH
FAYCETT, MO

These roll-ups are very fast to fix. I like that you can make them ahead and keep them wrapped in the refrigerator until you're ready to serve.

CHEESY ONION ROLL-UPS

PREP: 20 MIN. + CHILLING   YIELD: ABOUT 5 DOZEN

1 cup (8 ounces) sour cream

1 package (8 ounces) cream cheese, softened

1/2 cup finely shredded cheddar cheese

3/4 cup sliced green onions

1 tablespoon lime juice

1 tablespoon minced seeded jalapeno pepper

1 package (10 ounces) flour tortillas (6 inches), warmed

Picante sauce

> In a large bowl, combine the first six ingredients. Spread over each tortilla and roll up tightly. Wrap and refrigerate for at least 1 hour. Slice into 1-in. pieces. Serve with picante sauce.

Editor's Note: When cutting hot peppers, disposable gloves are recommended. Avoid touching your face.

tips&ideas

Following a few simple tips will help you host a successful appetizer buffet. Here's one to keep in mind: Because people are more inclined to eat something when they know exactly what it is, consider labeling the appetizers with place cards.

MARY BETH HARRIS-MURPHREE
TYLER, TX

Filled with a tasty sweet potato mixture, these delicious baked wraps are a favorite of vegetarians or anyone trying to choose healthier snacks. Served with salsa, they're sure to vanish from appetizer trays very quickly.

CRISPY CARIBBEAN VEGGIE WRAPS

PREP: 40 MIN. BAKE: 15 MIN. YIELD: 22 APPETIZERS

1 medium sweet potato

1/2 cup canned black beans, rinsed and drained

1/4 cup chopped red onion

2 tablespoons minced fresh cilantro

1 tablespoon lime juice

1 teaspoon salt

1 teaspoon ground cumin

1 teaspoon chopped jalapeno pepper

1 garlic clove, minced

1/4 cup water

22 wonton wrappers

1-1/2 cups salsa

> Scrub sweet potato and pierce with a fork; place on a microwave-safe plate. Microwave, uncovered, on high for 12-14 minutes or until tender, turning once. Cool. Slit potato and scoop pulp into a small bowl. Mash pulp; stir in the beans, onion, cilantro, lime juice, salt, cumin, jalapeno and garlic.

> Lightly brush water over all four edges of one wonton wrapper. (Keep wrappers covered with a damp paper towel until ready to use.) Spread 1 tablespoon filling along one edge of wrapper; roll up tightly. Repeat with remaining wrappers and filling.

> Place on a baking sheet coated with cooking spray. Lightly spray wraps with cooking spray. Bake at 375° for 15 minutes or until golden brown. Serve warm with salsa.

Editor's Note: This recipe was tested in a 1,100-watt microwave. When cutting hot peppers, disposable gloves are recommended. Avoid touching your face.

TURKEY EGG ROLLS

PREP/TOTAL TIME: 30 MIN. YIELD: 10 EGG ROLLS

LUCILLE GENDRON PELHAM, NH

Coleslaw mix hurries along the preparation of these deep-fried egg rolls served with sweet-and-sour sauce. The savory starters are as easy to make as they are to eat.

1/2 pound ground turkey

2 cups coleslaw mix

1 tablespoon soy sauce

1/2 teaspoon ground ginger

1/4 teaspoon onion salt

1/4 teaspoon garlic powder

10 egg roll wrappers

Oil for frying

Sweet-and-sour sauce

> In a large skillet, cook turkey over medium heat until no longer pink; drain. Stir in the coleslaw mix, soy sauce, ginger, onion salt and garlic powder. Place 1/4 cup in the center of each egg roll wrapper. Fold bottom corner over filling; fold sides toward center. Moisten remaining corner of wrapper with water; roll up tightly to seal. Repeat.

> In an electric skillet or deep-fat fryer, heat oil to 375°. Fry egg rolls, a few at a time, for 3-4 minutes or until golden brown, turning often. Drain on paper towels. Serve with sweet-and-sour sauce.

CHICKEN TURNOVERS

PREP/TOTAL TIME: 30 MIN. YIELD: 8 SERVINGS

SANDRA LEE HERR STEVENS, PA

Here's a great way to use up leftover chicken. The savory, cheesy bites make a great party starter, but sometimes, I serve them with fruit salad for a delicious, light meal.

1 cup diced cooked chicken breast

1 cup (4 ounces) shredded reduced-fat cheddar cheese

1/4 cup chopped celery

1 tablespoon finely chopped onion

1/4 teaspoon salt

1/4 teaspoon pepper

1 tube (8 ounces) refrigerated reduced-fat crescent rolls

> In a small bowl, combine the chicken, cheese, celery, onion, salt and pepper. Separate crescent dough into eight triangles; top each with chicken mixture. Fold dough over and seal edges.

> Place on an ungreased baking sheet. Bake at 375° for 13-17 minutes or until golden brown. Serve warm.

tips&ideas

When all of the serving dishes on a buffet table are at the same height, the table can look a little flat. Fix that by gathering phone books, buckets, hardcover books or sturdy boxes and arrange them on the table. Then drape a tablecloth over the "risers." Instant visual interest!

VEGGIE SHRIMP EGG ROLLS

PREP: 45 MIN. + STANDING   COOK: 10 MIN./BATCH
YIELD: 38 EGG ROLLS

CAROLE RESNICK CLEVELAND, OH
These wonderful starters will be the hit of your next party. The apricot dipping sauce comes together in a pinch.

2 teaspoons minced fresh gingerroot

1 garlic clove, minced

3 tablespoons olive oil, divided

1/2 pound uncooked medium shrimp, peeled, deveined and chopped

2 green onions, finely chopped

1 medium carrot, finely chopped

1 medium sweet red pepper, finely chopped

1 cup canned bean sprouts, rinsed and finely chopped

2 tablespoons water

2 tablespoons reduced-sodium soy sauce

38 wonton wrappers

APRICOT-MUSTARD DIPPING SAUCE:

3/4 cup apricot spreadable fruit

1 tablespoon water

1 tablespoon lime juice

1 tablespoon reduced-sodium soy sauce

1-1/2 teaspoons Dijon mustard

1/4 teaspoon minced fresh gingerroot

> In a large skillet, saute ginger and garlic in 1 tablespoon oil over medium heat until tender. Add shrimp, onions, carrot, red pepper, bean sprouts, water and soy sauce; cook and stir for 2-3 minutes or until vegetables are crisp-tender and shrimp turn pink. Reduce heat to low; cook for 4-5 minutes or until most of the liquid has evaporated. Remove from the heat; let stand for 15 minutes.

> Place a tablespoonful of shrimp mixture in the center of a wonton wrapper. (Keep wrappers covered with a damp paper towel until ready to use.) Fold bottom corner over filling. Fold sides toward center over filling. Moisten remaining corner with water; roll up tightly to seal.

> In a large skillet over medium heat, cook egg rolls, a few at a time, in remaining oil for 5-7 minutes on each side or until golden brown. Drain on paper towels.

> In a blender, combine the sauce ingredients; cover and process until smooth. Serve with egg rolls.

RANCH TORTILLA ROLL-UPS

PREP: 10 MIN. + CHILLING   YIELD: 16 SERVINGS

KAREN THOMAS BERLIN, PA
These zesty roll-ups are great as picnic nibbles, dinner appetizers and football party munchies. When my husband's co-workers at the state patrol come over for meals, they admit that "low-fat" can be delicious.

2 packages (8 ounces each) fat-free cream cheese

1 envelope ranch salad dressing mix

2 to 3 jalapeno peppers, finely chopped

1 jar (2 ounces) diced pimientos, drained

8 flour tortillas (8 inches)

> In a small bowl, combine the cream cheese, salad dressing mix, jalapenos and pimientos. Spread over tortillas. Roll up tightly; wrap each in plastic wrap. Refrigerate for at least 1 hour. Unwrap and cut each tortilla into eight pieces.

Editor's Note: When cutting hot peppers, disposable gloves are recommended. Avoid touching your face.

TASTE OF HOME
TEST KITCHEN
GREENDALE, WI

These tasty wraps cut fat as well as cleanup by keeping the deep fryer at bay. Our home economists filled the savory bundles with turkey sausage, garlic and onion.

MINI SAUSAGE BUNDLES

PREP/TOTAL TIME: 30 MIN. YIELD: 1 DOZEN

1/2 pound turkey Italian sausage links, casings removed

1 small onion, finely chopped

1/4 cup finely chopped sweet red pepper

1 garlic clove, minced

1/2 cup shredded cheddar cheese

8 sheets phyllo dough (14 inches x 9 inches)

12 whole chives, optional

> Crumble the sausage into a large nonstick skillet; add onion, red pepper and garlic. Cook over medium heat until meat is no longer pink; drain. Stir in cheese; cool slightly.

> Place one sheet of phyllo dough on a work surface; coat with cooking spray. Cover with a second sheet of phyllo: coat with cooking spray. (Until ready to use, keep remaining phyllo covered with plastic wrap and a damp towel to prevent drying out.) Cut widthwise into three 4-in. strips, discarding trimmings. Top each with 2 rounded tablespoons of sausage mixture; fold bottom and side edges over filling and roll up. Repeat with remaining phyllo and filling.

> Place seam side down on an ungreased baking sheet. Bake at 425° for 5-6 minutes or until lightly browned. Tie a chive around each bundle if desired. Serve warm.

KATE DAMPIER
QUAIL VALLEY, CA

My popular pinwheels wow guests at holiday parties I attend. People like the smokiness of the ham and the sweet surprise of the cherries. I appreciate the make-ahead convenience.

BLACK FOREST HAM PINWHEELS

PREP: 20 MIN. + CHILLING YIELD: ABOUT 3-1/2 DOZEN

1 package (8 ounces) cream cheese, softened

4 teaspoons minced fresh dill

1 tablespoon lemon juice

2 teaspoons Dijon mustard

Dash salt and pepper

1/2 cup dried cherries, chopped

1/4 cup chopped green onions

5 flour tortillas (10 inches), room temperature

1/2 pound sliced deli Black Forest ham

1/2 pound sliced Swiss cheese

> In a small bowl, beat the cream cheese, dill, lemon juice, mustard, salt and pepper until blended. Stir in the cherries and onions. Spread over each tortilla; layer with ham and cheese.

> Roll up tightly; wrap in plastic wrap. Refrigerate for at least 2 hours. Cut into 1/2-in. slices.

tips&ideas

Have an opened package of tortillas in the refrigerator? Here's a sweet way to use up the extra. Brush the tortillas with butter and sprinkle with fresh herbs or cinnamon-sugar. Then bake on a cookie sheet until crisp. Enjoy!

CRANBERRY FETA PINWHEELS

PREP: 20 MIN. + CHILLING YIELD: 40 APPETIZERS

JOYCE BENNINGER OWEN SOUND, ON

These pretty nibbles will disappear so fast, you may want to make an extra batch! The dried cranberries and chopped green onions create the perfect flavor combination.

1 carton (8 ounces) whipped cream cheese, softened

1 cup (8 ounces) crumbled feta cheese

1/4 cup chopped green onions

1 package (6 ounces) dried cranberries

4 flour tortillas (10 inches)

> In a small bowl, combine the cream cheese, feta cheese and onions. Stir in cranberries. Spread about 1/2 cup mixture over each tortilla and roll up tightly. Wrap with plastic wrap and refrigerate for at least 1 hour. Cut each roll-up into 10 slices.

ASIAN SPRING ROLLS

PREP: 40 MIN. COOK: 10 MIN.
YIELD: 8 SPRING ROLLS (1 CUP SAUCE)

NIRVANA HARRIS MUNDELEIN, IL

The slightly spicy peanut sauce that accompanies these fresh-tasting spring rolls really complements the traditional veggie-filled bites. They take some time to prepare but are worth it!

3 tablespoons lime juice

1 tablespoon hoisin sauce

1 teaspoon sugar

1 teaspoon salt

3 ounces uncooked Asian rice noodles

1 large carrot, grated

1 medium cucumber, peeled, seeded and julienned

1 medium jalapeno pepper, seeded and chopped

1/3 cup chopped dry roasted peanuts

8 spring roll wrappers or rice papers (8 inches)

1/2 cup loosely packed fresh cilantro

PEANUT SAUCE:

2 garlic cloves, minced

1/2 to 1 teaspoon crushed red pepper flakes

2 teaspoons canola oil

1/4 cup hoisin sauce

1/4 cup creamy peanut butter

2 tablespoons tomato paste

1/2 cup hot water

> In a small bowl, combine the lime juice, hoisin sauce and sugar; set aside. In a large saucepan, bring 2 qts. water and salt to a boil. Add noodles; cook for 2-3 minutes or until tender. Drain and rinse with cold water.

> Transfer to a large bowl and toss with 2 tablespoons reserved lime juice mixture; set aside. In another bowl, combine the carrot, cucumber, jalapeno and peanuts. Toss with the remaining lime juice mixture; set aside.

> Soak spring roll wrappers in cool water for 5 minutes. Carefully separate and place on a flat surface. Top each with several cilantro leaves. Place 1/4 cup carrot mixture and 1/4 cup noodles down the center of each wrapper to within 1-1/2 in. of ends.

> Fold both ends over filling; fold one long side over the filling, then carefully roll up tightly. Place seam side down on serving plate. Cover with damp paper towels until serving.

> In a small saucepan, cook garlic and pepper flakes in oil for 2 minutes. Add the remaining sauce ingredients; cook and stir until combined and thickened. Serve with spring rolls.

Editor's Note: When cutting hot peppers, disposable gloves are recommended. Avoid touching your face.

AUSSIE SAUSAGE ROLLS

PREP: 15 MIN. BAKE: 20 MIN. YIELD: 3 DOZEN

MELISSA LANDON PORT CHARLOTTE, FL

I was born and raised in Australia, but moved to the U.S. when I married my husband. When I long for a taste of home, I bake up these savory sausage rolls.

1-1/4 pounds bulk pork sausage

1 medium onion, finely chopped

2 teaspoons snipped chives

2 teaspoons minced fresh basil or 1/2 teaspoon dried basil

2 garlic cloves, minced

1 teaspoon paprika, divided

1/2 teaspoon salt

1/4 teaspoon pepper

1 package (17.3 ounces) frozen puff pastry, thawed

> In a large bowl, combine the sausage, onion, chives, basil, garlic, 3/4 teaspoon paprika, salt and pepper. Unfold pastry onto a lightly floured surface. Roll each pastry sheet into an 11-in. x 10-1/2-in. rectangle. Cut widthwise into 3-1/2-in. strips.

> Spread 1/2 cup of sausage mixture down the center of each strip. Fold pastry over and press edges together to seal. Cut each roll into six pieces. Place seam side down on a rack in a shallow baking pan. Sprinkle with remaining paprika.

> Bake rolls at 350° for 20-25 minutes or until golden brown.

RANCH PIZZA PINWHEELS

PREP/TOTAL TIME: 25 MIN. YIELD: 1 DOZEN

JENNIFER DIETZ FARGO, ND

I developed this appetizer to mimic a dish at one of my favorite restaurants. I often need to double the recipe because one batch disappears so quickly!

1 tube (13.8 ounces) refrigerated pizza crust

1/4 cup prepared ranch salad dressing

1/2 cup shredded Colby-Monterey Jack cheese

1/2 cup diced pepperoni

1/4 cup chopped green onions

Pizza sauce, warmed or additional ranch salad dressing, optional

> On a lightly floured surface, roll pizza dough into a 12-in. x 10-in. rectangle. Spread ranch dressing evenly to within 1/4 in. of edges. Sprinkle with cheese, pepperoni and onions. Roll up jelly-roll style, starting with a long side.

> Cut into 1-in. slices. Place cut side down on a greased baking sheet. Bake at 425° for 10-13 minutes or until lightly browned. Serve warm with pizza sauce or additional ranch dressing if desired. Refrigerate leftovers.

JENNIFER PFAFF
INDIANAPOLIS, IN

Mouth-watering Brie, succulent crab and a hint of pear make this delicate pastry a true favorite. The smooth, creamy Brie and flaky crust always melt in your mouth.

CRAB 'N' BRIE STRUDEL SLICES

PREP: 45 MIN. BAKE: 20 MIN. YIELD: 2 DOZEN

1/2 pound fresh crabmeat

6 ounces Brie or Camembert cheese, rind removed and cut into 1/4-inch cubes

2-1/2 cups finely chopped peeled ripe pears

1/2 cup thinly sliced green onions

1/2 cup diced fully cooked ham

2 teaspoons lemon juice

1 garlic clove, minced

Dash pepper

14 sheets phyllo dough (14 inches x 9 inches)

3/4 cup butter, melted

> In a large bowl, combine the first eight ingredients; set aside.

> Place a piece of plastic wrap larger than a sheet of phyllo on a work surface. Place one phyllo sheet on plastic wrap; brush with butter. (Keep remaining phyllo covered until ready to use.) Repeat six times. Spread half of crab filling to within 1 in. of edges. Fold the two short sides over filling. Using the plastic wrap to lift one long side, roll up jelly-roll style.

> Transfer to a greased 15-in. x 10-in. baking pan; discard plastic wrap. Brush top with butter; score top lightly at 1-in. intervals. Repeat with remaining phyllo, butter and filling.

> Bake at 375° for 20-25 minutes or until golden brown. Let stand for 5 minutes. Cut into slices along scored lines.

KENDRA DOSS
SMITHVILLE, MO

Filled with chicken, mushrooms, water chestnuts and carrots, these wraps are both healthy and yummy. The gingerroot, rice wine vinegar and teriyaki sauce give them delicious Asian flair.

CHICKEN LETTUCE WRAPS

PREP/TOTAL TIME: 25 MIN. YIELD: 6 SERVINGS

1-1/2 pounds boneless skinless chicken breasts, cubed

1 tablespoon plus 1-1/2 teaspoons peanut oil, divided

3/4 cup chopped fresh mushrooms

1 can (8 ounces) water chestnuts, drained and diced

1 tablespoon minced fresh gingerroot

2 tablespoons rice vinegar

2 tablespoons reduced-sodium teriyaki sauce

1 tablespoon reduced-sodium soy sauce

1/2 teaspoon garlic powder

1/4 teaspoon crushed red pepper flakes

1-1/2 cups shredded carrots

1/2 cup julienned green onions

12 Bibb or Boston lettuce leaves

1/3 cup sliced almonds, toasted

> In a large nonstick skillet coated with cooking spray, cook chicken in 1 tablespoon oil for 3 minutes; drain. Add the mushrooms, water chestnuts and ginger; cook 4-6 minutes longer or until chicken juices run clear. Drain and set aside.

> In a small bowl, whisk the vinegar, teriyaki sauce, soy sauce, garlic powder, red pepper flakes and remaining oil. Stir in the carrots, onions and chicken mixture. Spoon onto lettuce leaves; sprinkle with almonds. If desired, fold sides of lettuce over filling and roll up.

tips&ideas

Fresh gingerroot lends a wonderful flavor to Asian-inspired appetizers such as Chicken Lettuce Wraps. You can find gingerroot in your grocer's produce section. It should have a smooth skin. To use, place it in the freezer for a bit. Fresh gingerroot is easier to peel and grate once it is frozen.

JALAPENO CHICKEN WRAPS

PREP: 15 MIN. GRILL: 20 MIN. YIELD: 2-1/2 DOZEN

LESLIE BUENZ TINLEY PARK, IL

These sizzling bites are always a hit at parties! Zesty strips of chicken and bits of onion sit in jalapeno halves that are wrapped in bacon and grilled. Serve them with blue cheese or ranch salad dressing for dipping.

1 pound boneless skinless chicken breasts

1 tablespoon garlic powder

1 tablespoon onion powder

1 tablespoon pepper

2 teaspoons seasoned salt

1 teaspoon paprika

1 small onion, cut into strips

15 jalapeno peppers, halved and seeded

1 pound sliced bacon, halved widthwise

Blue cheese salad dressing

> Cut chicken into 2-in. x 1-1/2-in. strips. In a large resealable plastic bag, combine the garlic powder, onion powder, pepper, seasoned salt and paprika; add chicken and shake to coat. Place a chicken and onion strip in each jalapeno half. Wrap each with a piece of bacon and secure with toothpicks.

> Grill, uncovered, over indirect medium heat for 9-10 minutes on each side or until chicken is no longer pink and bacon is crisp. Serve with blue cheese dressing.

Editor's Note: When cutting hot peppers, disposable gloves are recommended. Avoid touching your face.

TURKEY TORTILLA SPIRALS

PREP: 25 MIN. + CHILLING YIELD: 3 DOZEN

PEGGY GRIEME PINEHURST, NC

No one suspects that these addictive pinwheels are light...or how easy they are to prepare. Both qualities make this yummy snack a winner in my kitchen.

3/4 pound thinly sliced deli turkey

6 flour tortillas (8 inches), room temperature

1 package (8 ounces) fat-free cream cheese

6 tablespoons finely chopped pecans

1 can (16 ounces) whole-berry cranberry sauce, divided

1/4 cup chopped celery

2 green onions, thinly sliced

> Place turkey on tortillas to within 1/4 in. of edge. Spread cream cheese over turkey; sprinkle with pecans. Spread each with 2 tablespoons cranberry sauce. Roll up jelly-roll style; wrap tightly in plastic wrap. Refrigerate for 1 hour or until firm.

> Just before serving, cut each roll into six pieces. In a small bowl, combine the celery, onions and remaining cranberry sauce. Serve with tortilla spirals.

stuffed butterflied shrimp, p. 57

Mix, mingle and munch your way to a winning party with this selection of substantial bites. These robust flavors and tempting textures satisfy the biggest appetites.

hot & hearty

GAIL PONAK
VISCOUNT, SK

These bite-sized chicken kabobs are a perfect appetizer. They are quick and easy to prepare, which means I can spend more time mingling with guests.

APPETIZER CHICKEN KABOBS

PREP: 15 MIN. + MARINATING BAKE: 10 MIN. YIELD: 20-24 APPETIZERS

3/4 cup soy sauce

1/4 cup sugar

1 tablespoon canola oil

1/4 teaspoon garlic powder

1/2 teaspoon ground ginger

2 boneless skinless chicken breasts, cut into 1-inch chunks

6 to 8 green onions, cut into 1-inch pieces

1/2 pound medium fresh mushrooms, stems removed

> In a large bowl, combine first five ingredients. Pour half into another bowl. Add chicken to one bowl and the onions to another bowl. Marinate for 30 minutes.

> Drain and discard marinade from chicken. Drain and reserve marinade from onions. On soaked wooden skewers, thread a piece of chicken, onion, mushroom and another chicken piece.

> Place on a broiler rack. Broil 5 in. from the heat, turning and basting with reserved marinade after 3 minutes. Broil for 3 minutes longer or until chicken juices run clear. Serve immediately.

GLAZED KIELBASA

PREP: 5 MIN. COOK: 4 HOURS YIELD: 12-16 SERVINGS

JODY SANDS TAYLOR RICHMOND, VA

You'll need only three ingredients to prepare this pleasantly sweet treatment for sausage. Serve with toothpicks for a filling appetizer or alone as a simple entree. To lighten up the recipe, fat-free or turkey kielbasa can be used instead.

3 pounds smoked kielbasa or Polish sausage, cut into 1-inch chunks

1/2 cup packed brown sugar

1-1/2 cups ginger ale

> Place sausage in a 3-qt. slow cooker; sprinkle with brown sugar. Pour ginger ale over the top. Cover and cook on low for 4-5 hours or until heated through. Serve with a slotted spoon.

HOT WINGS

PREP: 15 MIN. BAKE: 1 HOUR YIELD: ABOUT 6 DOZEN

CORALIE BEGIN FAIRFIELD, ME

These appetizers are a hearty choice—with just the right amount of "heat." Because my family enjoys them so much, I sometimes make enough to serve them as our main course.

7 to 8 pounds fresh or frozen chicken wingettes, thawed

4 cups ketchup

2-1/2 cups packed brown sugar

1-1/3 cups water

1 cup Louisiana-style hot sauce

1/3 cup Worcestershire sauce

2-1/2 teaspoons chili powder

2 teaspoons garlic powder

1/2 teaspoon onion powder

> Place the chicken wings in two greased 15-in. x 10-in. baking pans. In a large bowl, combine the remaining ingredients. Pour over wings.

> Bake, uncovered, at 350° for 1 hour or until chicken juices run clear. Spoon sauce from pans over wings if desired.

tips&ideas

If using a slow cooker to prepare a recipe, refrain from lifting the lid while the food is simmering unless the recipe instructs you to stir in or add ingredients. The loss of steam can mean an additional 15 to 30 minutes of cooking each time you lift the lid.

> Meanwhile, in a large skillet, combine glaze ingredients and reserved pineapple juice. Add meatballs. Bring to a boil over medium heat. Reduce heat; cook and stir for 5-10 minutes or until heated through.

GRILLED PORK SKEWERS

PREP: 10 MIN. + MARINATING   GRILL: 10 MIN.   YIELD: 8 SERVINGS

SUSAN LEBRUN SULPHUR, LA

People never seem to get enough of these tender hors d'oeuvres. Marinated in an Asian-inspired sauce that's slightly sweetened with honey, the flavorful party starters also make a wonderful entree when served over rice.

1 pound boneless whole pork loin roast

3 tablespoons reduced-sodium soy sauce

3 tablespoons honey

1 tablespoon lemon juice

1 tablespoon canola oil

3 garlic cloves, minced

1/2 teaspoon ground ginger

> Cut pork into 1/8-in. slices, then cut each slice widthwise in half. In a large resealable plastic bag, combine the remaining ingredients; add pork. Seal bag and turn to coat; refrigerate for 2-4 hours, turning occasionally.

> If grilling the kabobs, coat grill rack with cooking spray before starting the grill. Drain and discard marinade. Thread pork onto metal or soaked wooden skewers.

> Grill, uncovered, over medium heat or broil 4-6 in. from the heat for 2-3 minutes on each side or until meat is no longer pink.

APPETIZER MEATBALLS

PREP/TOTAL TIME: 30 MIN. YIELD: 4 DOZEN

KAREN MELLINGER BAKER DOVER, OH

I blend a can of crushed pineapple into these meatballs to create a taste-tempting treat. The sweet and tangy glaze that coats the bite-size snacks is a snap to prepare.

1 can (8 ounces) crushed pineapple

1 egg

1/4 cup dry bread crumbs

1/8 teaspoon pepper

1/2 pound bulk pork sausage

1/2 pound ground beef

GLAZE:

1/4 cup packed brown sugar

1/4 cup ketchup

1/4 cup white vinegar

1/4 cup water

2 tablespoons Dijon-mayonnaise blend

> Drain pineapple, reserving juice. Place pineapple and 2 tablespoons juice in a large bowl (set the remaining juice aside for glaze). Add the egg, bread crumbs and pepper to pineapple. Stir in sausage and beef. Shape into 1-in. balls.

> Place meatballs on a greased rack in a shallow baking pan. Bake, uncovered, at 450° for 12-15 minutes or until no longer pink; drain.

tips&ideas —— *Make perfectly sized Appetizer Meatballs by lightly patting the meat mixture into a 1-in.-thick rectangle. Cut the rectangle into the same number of squares as meatballs needed and roll each square into a ball.*

MARY PLUMMER
DE SOTO, KS

Whether you need a fun appetizer or a tasty side dish, turn to these potato skins topped with Canadian bacon, chopped tomato and reduced-fat cheese.

CANADIAN BACON POTATO SKINS

PREP: 30 MIN. BAKE: 15 MIN. YIELD: 8 SERVINGS

6 large baking potatoes
(12 ounces each)

2 teaspoons canola oil

1/8 teaspoon hot pepper sauce

1 teaspoon chili powder

1 medium tomato, seeded and
finely chopped

2/3 cup chopped Canadian bacon

2 tablespoons finely chopped
green onion

1 cup (4 ounces) shredded
reduced-fat cheddar cheese

1/2 cup reduced-fat sour cream

> Place potatoes on a microwave-safe plate; prick with a fork. Microwave, uncovered, on high for 14-17 minutes or until tender but firm, turning once. Let stand for 5 minutes.

> Cut each potato in half lengthwise. Scoop out pulp, leaving a 1/4-in. shell (discard pulp or save for another use).

> Combine oil and pepper sauce; brush over potato shells. Sprinkle with chili powder. Cut each potato shell in half lengthwise. Place on baking sheets coated with cooking spray. Sprinkle with the tomato, bacon, onion and cheese.

> Bake at 450° for 12-14 minutes or until heated through and cheese is melted. Serve with sour cream.

Editor's Note: This recipe was tested in a 1,100-watt microwave.

GAIL CAWSEY
FAWNSKIN, CA

Here's a snack that's a simple crowd-pleaser. Rotisserie chicken keeps it quick, while the seasonings and lime juice add vibrant flavor.

BAKED CHICKEN NACHOS

PREP: 20 MIN. BAKE: 15 MIN. YIELD: 16 SERVINGS

2 medium sweet red peppers, diced

1 medium green pepper, diced

3 teaspoons canola oil, divided

1 can (15 ounces) black beans, rinsed and drained

1 teaspoon minced garlic

1 teaspoon dried oregano

1/4 teaspoon ground cumin

2-1/4 cups shredded cooked rotisserie chicken

4-1/2 teaspoons lime juice

1/8 teaspoon salt

1/8 teaspoon pepper

7-1/2 cups tortilla chips

8 ounces pepper Jack cheese, shredded

1/4 cup thinly sliced green onions

1/2 cup minced fresh cilantro

1 cup (8 ounces) sour cream

2 to 3 teaspoons diced pickled jalapeno peppers, optional

> In a large skillet, saute peppers in 1-1/2 teaspoons oil for 3 minutes or until crisp-tender; transfer to a small bowl. In the same skillet, saute the beans, garlic, oregano and cumin in remaining oil for 3 minutes or until heated through.

> Meanwhile, combine the chicken, lime juice, salt and pepper. In a greased 13-in. x 9-in. baking dish, layer half of the tortilla chips, pepper mixture, bean mixture, chicken, cheese, onions and cilantro. Repeat layers.

> Bake, uncovered, at 350° for 15-20 minutes or until heated through. Serve with sour cream and pickled jalapenos if desired.

tips&ideas

With its slightly sharp flavor, cilantro gives a distinctive taste to Mexican, Latin American and Asian dishes. Like all other fresh herbs, cilantro should be used as soon as possible. For short-term storage, immerse freshly cut stems in water about 2 inches deep. Cover leaves loosely with a plastic bag and refrigerate for several days. Wash just before using.

HEARTY POPPERS

PREP: 35 MIN. BAKE: 20 MIN. YIELD: 2 DOZEN

JANICE VERNON LAS CRUCES, NM

There are many recipes for jalapeno pepper poppers where we live; but for a potluck at our church, my husband and I came up with this lighter—but equally delicious—version. The spicy bites were a huge hit!

12 jalapeno peppers

1/2 pound lean ground turkey

1/4 cup finely chopped onion

4 ounces fat-free cream cheese

1-1/3 cups shredded part-skim mozzarella cheese, divided

1 tablespoon minced fresh cilantro

1 teaspoon chili powder

1/2 teaspoon garlic powder

1/2 teaspoon ground cumin

1/8 teaspoon salt

1/8 teaspoon pepper

> Cut jalapenos in half lengthwise, leaving stems intact; discard seeds. Set aside. In a small nonstick skillet over medium heat, cook turkey and onion until meat is no longer pink; drain.

> In a small bowl, combine the cream cheese, 1/3 cup cheese, cilantro, chili powder, garlic powder, cumin, salt and pepper. Stir in turkey mixture. Spoon generously into pepper halves.

> Place in a 15-in. x 10-in. baking pan coated with cooking spray; sprinkle with remaining cheese. Bake, uncovered, at 350° for 20 minutes for spicy flavor, 30 minutes for medium flavor and 40 minutes for mild flavor.

Editor's Note: When cutting hot peppers, disposable gloves are recommended. Avoid touching your face.

MINI HOT DOGS 'N' MEATBALLS

PREP: 5 MIN. COOK: 3 HOURS YIELD: 8 CUPS

ANDREA CHAMBERLAIN MACEDON, NY

Hot appetizers don't come much easier than this...and the flavorful nibbles appeal to all ages. Feel free to vary the meats to suit your family's tastes, or increase the heat factor by using a spicier barbecue sauce.

36 frozen cooked Italian meatballs (1/2 ounce each)

1 package (16 ounces) miniature hot dogs or smoked sausages

1 package (3-1/2 ounces) sliced pepperoni

1 jar (26 ounces) meatless spaghetti sauce

1 bottle (18 ounces) barbecue sauce

1 bottle (12 ounces) chili sauce

> In a 5-qt. slow cooker, combine all ingredients. Cover and cook on low for 3 hours or until heated through.

BREADED RAVIOLI

PREP: 20 MIN. + STANDING BAKE: 10 MIN. YIELD: 6 SERVINGS

MICHELLE SMITH SYKESVILLE, MD

These lightly breaded ravioli are baked instead of deep-fried to be much kinder to your waistline. The homemade tomato and green pepper salsa is the best I've ever tried.

1 package (16 ounces) frozen beef ravioli

1/2 cup dry bread crumbs

1/2 to 1-1/2 teaspoons salt-free Italian herb seasoning

1/4 cup reduced-fat Italian salad dressing

ITALIAN SALSA:

1 can (14-1/2 ounces) diced tomatoes, undrained

1/2 medium green pepper, quartered

1/2 small red onion, quartered

1 tablespoon minced fresh oregano or 1 teaspoon dried oregano

1 tablespoon minced fresh basil or 1 teaspoon dried basil

1 garlic clove, minced

1 teaspoon balsamic vinegar

1/2 teaspoon salt

1/4 teaspoon sugar

> Cook ravioli according to package directions; drain and let stand for 10 minutes. In a shallow bowl, combine bread crumbs and seasoning. In another shallow bowl, pour dressing. Dip ravioli into dressing, then coat with crumb mixture.

> Place on baking sheets coated with cooking spray. Lightly coat ravioli with cooking spray. Bake at 400° for 8-9 minutes or until lightly browned.

> Meanwhile, in a food processor, combine the salsa ingredients. Pulse for 15-20 seconds. Serve ravioli with salsa.

CHICKEN BACON BITES

PREP: 15 MIN. + MARINATING BROIL: 10 MIN. YIELD: 2 DOZEN

BETTY PIERSON WELLINGTON, FL

Ginger and orange marmalade give these rumaki-style snacks wonderful flavor. I marinate the wrapped chicken earlier in the day and broil them when guests arrive.

12 bacon strips, halved

10 ounces boneless skinless chicken breasts, cut into 24 cubes

1 can (8 ounces) sliced water chestnuts, drained

1/2 cup orange marmalade

1/4 cup soy sauce

2 garlic cloves, minced

1 teaspoon grated fresh gingerroot

Sweet-and-sour sauce, optional

> Place bacon on a broiler rack. Broil 4 in. from the heat for 1-2 minutes on each side or until partially cooked; cool.

> Wrap a piece of bacon around a chicken cube and water chestnut slice; secure with a toothpick. In a large resealable plastic bag, combine the orange marmalade, soy sauce, garlic and ginger. Add wrapped chicken; seal and carefully turn to coat. Refrigerate for 2 hours.

> Drain and discard marinade. Broil chicken for 3-4 minutes on each side or until chicken is no longer pink and bacon is crisp. Serve warm with the sweet-and-sour sauce if desired.

tips&ideas

While dry bread crumbs may be purchased at the store, you can also make your own using very dry bread or zwieback crackers. Place the bread or crackers in a plastic bag and crush with a rolling pin. Spoon the desired amount of crumbs into a measuring cup.

TASTE OF HOME
TEST KITCHEN
GREENDALE, WI

With a crispy coconut-cilantro coating and a sweet apricot dipping sauce, these delicious shrimp created by our home economists are a great choice for any special event.

COCONUT SHRIMP WITH DIPPING SAUCE

PREP: 1-1/4 HOURS + MARINATING BAKE: 15 MIN. YIELD: 5 SERVINGS

1 can (14 ounces) light coconut milk, divided

1 jalapeno pepper, seeded and chopped

1/4 cup minced fresh cilantro

1-1/4 pounds uncooked medium shrimp

3/4 cup all-purpose flour

4 egg whites

3/4 cup panko (Japanese) bread crumbs

3/4 cup flaked coconut, lightly toasted

1/3 cup reduced-sugar apricot preserves

1 teaspoon spicy brown mustard

> Place 2 tablespoons coconut milk in a small bowl; cover and refrigerate. In a large resealable plastic bag, combine the jalapeno, cilantro and remaining coconut milk. Peel and devein shrimp, leaving tails on. Add to bag; seal and turn to coat. Refrigerate for 1 hour.

> Place flour in a shallow bowl. In another bowl, lightly beat the egg whites. In a third bowl, combine bread crumbs and coconut. Drain and discard marinade. Dip shrimp in flour and egg whites, then roll in crumb mixture.

> Place on a baking sheet coated with cooking spray. Bake at 400° for 7-9 minutes on each side or until lightly browned. Meanwhile, for dipping sauce, add preserves and mustard to the reserved coconut milk. Serve with shrimp.

Editor's Note: When cutting hot peppers, disposable gloves are recommended. Avoid touching your face.

LILY-MICHELE ALEXIS
LOUISVILLE, KY

When you want to add a "meaty" option to your appetizer buffet, look no further than these finger-licking-good ribs! The honey-garlic flavor is divine!

HONEY GARLIC RIBS

PREP: 15 MIN. BAKE: 2-1/4 HOURS YIELD: 24 SERVINGS

6 pounds pork baby back ribs, cut into two-rib portions

2 cups water, divided

3/4 cup packed brown sugar

2 tablespoons cornstarch

1 teaspoon garlic powder

1/4 teaspoon ground ginger

1/4 cup soy sauce

1/2 cup honey

> Place ribs bone side down in a large roasting pan; pour 1 cup of water over ribs. Cover tightly and bake at 350° for 1-1/2 hours.

> In a small bowl, combine the brown sugar, cornstarch, garlic powder and ginger. Stir in the soy sauce, honey and remaining water until smooth. Drain fat from roasting pan; pour sauce over ribs.

> Bake, uncovered, for 45 minutes or until meat is tender.

NUTTY STUFFED MUSHROOMS

PREP/TOTAL TIME: 30 MIN. YIELD: 18-20 SERVINGS

MILDRED ELDRED UNION CITY, MI

Basil, Parmesan cheese and mushrooms blend together well, while buttery pecans give these treats a surprising crunch.

18 to 20 large fresh mushrooms

1 small onion, chopped

3 tablespoons butter

1/4 cup dry bread crumbs

1/4 cup finely chopped pecans

3 tablespoons grated Parmesan cheese

1/4 teaspoon salt

1/4 teaspoon dried basil

Dash cayenne pepper

> Remove stems from mushrooms; set caps aside. Finely chop stems. In a large skillet, saute chopped mushrooms and onion in butter for 5 minutes or until liquid has evaporated. Remove from the heat; set aside.

> In a small bowl, combine the bread crumbs, pecans, Parmesan cheese, salt, basil and cayenne; add mushroom mixture. Stuff firmly into mushroom caps.

> Place in a greased 15-in. x 10-in. baking pan. Bake, uncovered, at 400° for 15-18 minutes or until tender. Serve warm.

PROSCIUTTO-WRAPPED APRICOTS

PREP/TOTAL TIME: 30 MIN. YIELD: 2 DOZEN

TASTE OF HOME TEST KITCHEN GREENDALE, WI

Our home economists stuffed dried apricots with sweetened Mascarpone cheese, then wrapped them with prosciutto before baking. The appealing snack is suitable for any occasion.

3/4 cup Mascarpone cheese

2 tablespoons confectioners' sugar

1/8 teaspoon white pepper

1 package (6 ounces) dried pitted Mediterranean apricots

12 thin slices prosciutto

> In a small bowl, combine the Mascarpone cheese, confectioners' sugar and pepper. Cut a slit in each apricot; fill with cheese mixture. Cut each slice of prosciutto in half lengthwise; wrap a piece around each apricot and secure with a toothpick.

> Place in an ungreased 15-in. x 10-in. baking pan. Bake, uncovered, at 425° for 15-20 minutes or until heated through. Refrigerate leftovers.

3 tablespoons butter, melted

2 tablespoons soy sauce

1 tablespoon lemon juice

1 tablespoon honey

1/2 teaspoon ground ginger

1/4 to 1/2 teaspoon crushed red pepper flakes

> Flatten chicken to 1/4-in. thickness; cut lengthwise into 1-in.-wide strips. In a large resealable plastic bag, combine the soy sauce, onion, sesame oil, brown sugar, honey, garlic and ginger; add chicken. Seal bag and turn to coat; refrigerate for 4 hours.

> In a food processor, combine the peanuts, onions and garlic; cover and process until mixture forms a paste. Add the broth, butter, soy sauce, lemon juice, honey, ginger and pepper flakes; cover and process until smooth. Transfer to a serving bowl. Refrigerate until serving.

> Drain and discard marinade. Thread chicken strips onto soaked wooden skewers. Broil 6 in. from the heat for 2-4 minutes on each side or until chicken is no longer pink. Serve with peanut sauce.

CHICKEN SATAY

PREP: 15 MIN. + MARINATING BROIL: 5 MIN.
YIELD: 10-12 SERVINGS

TASTE OF HOME TEST KITCHEN GREENDALE, WI
This Asian-style starter features tender strips of chicken and a simple-to-prepare peanut sauce.

2 pounds boneless skinless chicken breasts

1/3 cup soy sauce

1 green onion, sliced

2 tablespoons sesame oil

1 tablespoon brown sugar

1 tablespoon honey

2 garlic cloves, minced

1/2 teaspoon ground ginger

PEANUT SAUCE:

1/2 cup salted peanuts

1/4 cup chopped green onions

1 garlic clove, minced

3 tablespoons chicken broth

ORANGE-GLAZED SMOKIES

PREP/TOTAL TIME: 15 MIN. YIELD: ABOUT 4 DOZEN

JUDY WILSON SUN CITY WEST, AZ
I always receive compliments when I bring these tasty sausages to an event. The succulent bites can be whipped up in just minutes, and the tangy sauce is an instant conversation starter.

1 cup packed brown sugar

1 tablespoon all-purpose flour

1/4 cup orange juice concentrate

2 tablespoons prepared mustard

1 tablespoon cider vinegar

1 package (16 ounces) miniature smoked sausages

> In a large microwave-safe bowl, combine the first five ingredients. Add sausages; stir to coat. Cover and microwave on high for 3-4 minutes or until bubbly, stirring three times.

Editor's Note: This recipe was tested in a 1,100-watt microwave.

JOAN ELLIOTT
DEEP RIVER, CT

These elegant, baked shrimp can be an appetizer or entree. Leaving the tails on the shrimp adds to the presentation.

STUFFED BUTTERFLIED SHRIMP

PREP: 20 MIN. + STANDING BAKE: 20 MIN. YIELD: 2 DOZEN

24 uncooked unpeeled large shrimp

1 cup Italian salad dressing

1-1/2 cups seasoned bread crumbs

1 can (6-1/2 ounces) chopped clams, drained and minced

6 tablespoons butter, melted

1-1/2 teaspoons minced fresh parsley

> Peel shrimp, leaving tail section on. Make a deep cut along the top of each shrimp (do not cut all the way through); remove the vein. Place shrimp in a shallow dish; add salad dressing. Set aside for 20 minutes.

> Meanwhile, in a large bowl, combine the bread crumbs, clams, butter and parsley. Drain and discard salad dressing. Arrange shrimp in a greased 13-in. x 9-in. baking dish. Open shrimp and press flat; fill each with 1 tablespoon of crumb mixture. Bake, uncovered, at 350° for 20-25 minutes or until shrimp turn pink.

tips&ideas

Here's a no-mess, no-fuss way to mince fresh parsley. You won't even need to drag out the cutting board. Simply place the parsley sprigs in a small glass container and snip sprigs with kitchen shears until minced. Then use the amount called for in the recipe. Done!

zippy cranberry appetizer, p. 70

Bright garden-fresh tomatoes...delicate tea sandwiches...chilled, bite-size kabobs...marinated cheeses...nosh away on these finger-food favorites.

cool&tasty

remaining oil; set aside. In a small bowl, combine the mayonnaise, Parmesan cheese, milk, pesto and pepper. Mash garlic into pesto mixture; stir until combined.

> Alternately thread tortellini and tomatoes onto toothpicks. Serve with pesto dip. Refrigerate leftovers.

DEVILED EGGS

PREP/TOTAL TIME: 15 MIN. YIELD: 1 DOZEN

MARGARET SANDERS INDIANAPOLIS, IN

For variety, feel free to use different seasonings in the filling for these creamy deviled eggs. Piping the filling into the egg whites lends an elegant flair to their appearance.

6 hard-cooked eggs

2 tablespoons mayonnaise

1 teaspoon sugar

1 teaspoon white vinegar

1 teaspoon prepared mustard

1/2 teaspoon salt

Paprika

> Slice eggs in half lengthwise; remove yolks and set whites aside. In a small bowl, mash yolks with a fork. Add the mayonnaise, sugar, vinegar, mustard and salt; mix well. Stuff or pipe into egg whites. Sprinkle with paprika. Refrigerate until serving.

TORTELLINI APPETIZERS

PREP: 20 MIN. BAKE: 20 MIN. + COOLING
YIELD: ABOUT 2 DOZEN (1-1/2 CUPS DIP)

CHERYL LAMA ROYAL OAK, MI

The festive green and red of this appetizer make it a welcomed addition to your party's buffet table. Store-bought pesto keeps the dip's preparation fast. Sometimes I like to heat the garlic in a skillet and use skewers for a different look.

4 garlic cloves, peeled

2 tablespoons olive oil, divided

1 package (10 ounces) refrigerated spinach tortellini

1 cup mayonnaise

1/4 cup grated Parmesan cheese

1/4 cup milk

1/4 cup prepared pesto

1/8 teaspoon pepper

1 pint grape tomatoes

26 frilled toothpicks

> Place garlic cloves on a double thickness of heavy-duty foil; drizzle with 1 tablespoon oil. Wrap foil around garlic. Bake at 425° for 20-25 minutes or until tender. Cool for 10-15 minutes.

> Meanwhile, cook tortellini according to package directions; drain and rinse in cold water. Toss with

KIM MARIE VAN RHEENEN
MENDOTA, IL

I like to serve these savory mushrooms alongside crackers or sliced baguettes. You might like to vary the cheese or add some olives, artichokes or a touch of basil.

MARINATED MUSHROOMS AND CHEESE

PREP: 10 MIN. + MARINATING YIELD: 12-14 SERVINGS

1/2 cup sun-dried tomatoes (not packed in oil), julienned

1 cup boiling water

1/2 cup olive oil

1/2 cup white wine vinegar

2 garlic cloves, minced

1/2 teaspoon salt

1/2 pound sliced fresh mushrooms

8 ounces Monterey Jack cheese, cubed

> In a small bowl, combine the tomatoes and water. Let stand for 5 minutes; drain. In a large resealable plastic bag, combine the oil, vinegar, garlic and salt; add the tomatoes, mushrooms and cheese. Seal bag and toss to coat. Refrigerate for at least 4 hours before serving. Drain and discard marinade.

tips&ideas

Fresh mushrooms should be used within a few days of purchase. If that's not possible, you can blanch them, then freeze for up to 1 month. To blanch, slice mushrooms and bring 1 quart of water to a boil. Add the mushrooms and 1 tablespoon lemon juice; cook for 3 minutes. Immediately remove mushrooms with a slotted spoon and cool in ice water for 3 to 4 minutes. Drain and pack into freezer containers.

*Wonton wrappers
form pretty, crunchy
holders for a creamy
mixture of canned crab
and rich, dill-flavored
cream cheese.*

CRAB-STUFFED CONES

PREP: 30 MIN. BAKE: 10 MIN. + COOLING YIELD: 2 DOZEN

24 wonton wrappers

1/4 cup butter, melted

1 teaspoon dill weed, divided

1/4 teaspoon garlic salt

1 package (8 ounces) cream cheese, softened

1 tablespoon sour cream

1/2 teaspoon lemon juice

1 can (6 ounces) crabmeat, drained, flaked and cartilage removed

> Place a wonton wrapper on a work surface with one corner facing you; roll into a cone. Cut the open end with a sharp scissors until edge is even. Place a 1-in. foil ball in opening. Place seam side down on a greased baking sheet. Repeat with remaining wonton wrappers.

> Bake at 375° for 10 minutes or until golden brown. In a small bowl, combine the butter, 1/2 teaspoon dill and garlic salt. Brush over horns. Remove to a wire rack to cool completely. Remove foil balls.

> In a large bowl, beat cream cheese until smooth. Beat in sour cream, lemon juice and remaining dill until blended. Fold in crab meat.

> Transfer crab mixture to a pastry or plastic bag; cut a hole in the corner. Pipe the crab mixture into cooled horns.

POTATO SALAD BITES

PREP: 30 MIN. COOK: 15 MIN. + CHILLING YIELD: 16 APPETIZERS

STEPHANIE SHERIDAN PLAINFIELD, VT

Here's a fun and tasty way to serve a favorite party side dish as an appetizer. A potato-salad filling is stuffed inside potato shells for a truly unique and delicious bite-size snack.

10 small red potatoes

1/4 cup chopped pimiento-stuffed olives

2 teaspoons minced fresh parsley

1 teaspoon finely chopped onion

1/2 cup mayonnaise

1-3/4 teaspoons Dijon mustard

1/8 teaspoon pepper

1/4 teaspoon salt

Paprika

Parsley sprigs, optional

> Place the potatoes in a large saucepan and cover with water. Bring to a boil. Reduce heat; cover and cook for 12-15 minutes or until tender. Drain and immediately place potatoes in ice water; drain the potatoes and pat dry.

> Peel two potatoes; finely dice and place in a small bowl. Cut the remaining potatoes in half. With a melon baller, scoop out pulp, leaving a 3/8-in. shell; set shells aside. Dice pulp and add to the bowl. Stir in the olives, parsley and onion. Combine the mayonnaise, mustard and pepper; gently stir into potato mixture.

> Sprinkle potato shells with salt; stuff with potato salad. Sprinkle with paprika. Chill for at least 1 hour before serving. Garnish with parsley if desired.

tips&ideas

Make a few extra batches of Marinated Mozzarella and divide among small glass jars. Tuck each jar into a pretty basket along with a small loaf of bread or some crackers to give away as unique party favors. After eating the cheese, the oil can be used for cooking.

MARINATED MOZZARELLA

PREP: 15 MIN. + MARINATING YIELD: 8-10 SERVINGS

PEGGY CAIRO KENOSHA, WI

I come home with an empty container whenever I bring this dish to a party. The mouth-watering cheese cubes can be made ahead to free up time later. I often serve them with party picks for a festive look.

1/3 cup olive oil

1 tablespoon chopped oil-packed sun-dried tomatoes

1 tablespoon minced fresh parsley

1 teaspoon crushed red pepper flakes

1 teaspoon dried basil

1 teaspoon minced chives

1/4 teaspoon garlic powder

1 pound cubed part-skim mozzarella cheese

> In a large resealable plastic bag, combine the first seven ingredients; add cheese cubes. Seal bag and turn to coat; refrigerate for at least 30 minutes. Transfer cheese cubes with marinade to a serving dish; serve with toothpicks.

SHRIMP SALAD ON ENDIVE

PREP/TOTAL TIME: 20 MIN. YIELD: ABOUT 1-1/2 DOZEN

TASTE OF HOME TEST KITCHEN GREENDALE, WI

Our home economists make a simple-to-prepare shrimp salad and serve it on endive leaves for a from-the-sea version of lettuce wraps. It's an easy way to add elegant flair to your party's offering of appetizers.

1/3 cup mayonnaise

1/2 teaspoon lemon juice

1/4 teaspoon dill weed

1/4 teaspoon seafood seasoning

1/8 teaspoon salt

1/8 teaspoon pepper

1/2 pound cooked shrimp, chopped

1 green onion, sliced

2 tablespoons chopped celery

1 tablespoon diced pimientos

2 heads Belgian endive, separated into leaves

> In a small bowl, combine the first six ingredients. Stir in the shrimp, onion, celery and pimientos. Spoon 1 tablespoonful onto each endive leaf; arrange on a platter. Refrigerate until serving.

ARTICHOKE CAPRESE PLATTER

PREP/TOTAL TIME: 15 MIN. YIELD: 10-12 SERVINGS

MARGARET WILSON HEMET, CA

This classic Italian combination of mozzarella, tomatoes and basil is dressed up with marinated artichokes. It looks so lovely on a platter. Using fresh mozzarella is the key to its great taste.

2 jars (7-1/2 ounces each) marinated artichoke hearts

2 tablespoons red wine vinegar

2 tablespoons olive oil

6 plum tomatoes, sliced

2 balls (8 ounces each) fresh mozzarella cheese, halved and sliced

2 cups loosely packed fresh basil leaves

> Drain artichokes, reserving 1/2 cup marinade; cut artichokes in half. In a small bowl, whisk vinegar, oil and reserved marinade.

> On a large serving platter, arrange artichokes, tomatoes, mozzarella cheese and basil. Drizzle with vinaigrette. Serve immediately.

Editor's Note: Fresh mozzarella can be found in the deli section of most grocery stores.

JOANNE BOONE
DANVILLE, OH

These flavorful bites are so fun to make and eat. But what I love most is how simple they are to assemble the day before an event.

MARINATED SAUSAGE KABOBS

PREP: 20 MIN. + MARINATING YIELD: 3 DOZEN

1/4 cup olive oil

1 tablespoon white vinegar

1/2 teaspoon minced garlic

1/2 teaspoon dried basil

1/2 teaspoon dried oregano

12 ounces cheddar cheese, cut into 3/4-inch cubes

1 medium sweet red pepper, cut into 3/4-inch pieces

1 medium green pepper, cut into 3/4-inch pieces

1 can (6 ounces) pitted ripe olives, drained

4 ounces hard salami, cut into 3/4-inch cubes

> In a large resealable plastic bag, combine the first five ingredients; add the remaining ingredients. Seal bag and turn to coat; refrigerate for at least 4 hours. Drain and discard marinade.

> For each kabob, thread one piece each of cheese, pepper, olive and salami onto a toothpick.

tips&ideas

Minced garlic that you buy in a jar, garlic that has been finely chopped by hand and garlic that has been put through a garlic press can all be used interchangeably in recipes. Choose whichever is easiest and most convenient for you.

CRYSTAL WILLIAMS
BROOKLYN, NY

I adore the classic combination of ripe tomatoes, mozzarella and basil in these mini bites. It is the genuine taste of true garden freshness.

CAPRESE TOMATO BITES

PREP/TOTAL TIME: 30 MIN. YIELD: ABOUT 3-1/2 DOZEN

1 pint cherry tomatoes, halved

3 tablespoons heavy whipping cream

1/2 pound fresh mozzarella cheese, sliced

6 fresh basil leaves

1 garlic clove, minced

1 tablespoon balsamic vinegar

> Scoop out and discard pulp of cherry tomatoes. Invert tomatoes onto paper towels to drain.

> In a food processor, combine the cream, mozzarella cheese, basil and garlic; cover and process until blended.

> Cut a small hole in the corner of a pastry or heavy-duty resealable plastic bag. Fill with cheese mixture.

> Turn tomato halves over; drizzle with vinegar. Pipe cheese mixture into tomatoes. Refrigerate until serving.

HAM CREAM CHEESE BALLS

PREP/TOTAL TIME: 25 MIN. YIELD: ABOUT 5 DOZEN

JILL KIRBY CALHOUN, GA

It seems like I'm always hosting a shower, birthday or other celebration. When I am short on time, I turn to these mouth-watering individual cheese balls.

2 packages (8 ounces each) cream cheese, softened

1 package (2-1/2 ounces) thinly sliced deli ham, finely chopped

3 green onions, finely chopped

2 tablespoons Worcestershire sauce

1 cup finely chopped peanuts

Crackers and raw vegetables

> In a large bowl, combine the cream cheese, ham, onions and Worcestershire sauce. Shape into 3/4-in. balls. Roll in peanuts. Cover and refrigerate until serving. Serve with crackers and vegetables.

FRUIT AND CHEESE KABOBS

PREP/TOTAL TIME: 20 MIN. YIELD: 12 KABOBS (1-1/2 CUPS DIP)

TASTE OF HOME TEST KITCHEN GREENDALE, WI

This fruity snack, developed by our home economists, is easy to make ahead and carry to a picnic in the park, backyard barbecue or dinner party. The cinnamon-spiced yogurt dip adds that special touch everyone loves!

1 pint fresh strawberries, halved

1-1/2 cups green grapes

1 package (8 ounces) cheddar and Monterey Jack cheese cubes

1 cup (8 ounces) vanilla yogurt

1/2 cup sour cream

2 tablespoons honey

1/2 teaspoon ground cinnamon

> On 12 wooden skewers, alternately thread the strawberries, grapes and cheese cubes. For dip, in a small bowl, combine the yogurt, sour cream, honey and cinnamon. Serve kabobs immediately or refrigerate until serving.

tips&ideas

If the word "chopped" comes before the ingredient when listed in a recipe, chop the ingredient before measuring. Using the example of "1 cup finely chopped peanuts" as listed in Ham Cream Cheese Balls, you should chop the peanuts and then measure 1 cup.

ZESTY MARINATED SHRIMP

PREP: 5 MIN. + CHILLING YIELD: 12 SERVINGS

MARY JANE GUEST ALAMOSA, CO

These easy shrimp look impressive and taste even better! The zesty sauce has a wonderful, spicy citrus flavor. I especially like this recipe because I can prepare it ahead of time.

1/2 cup canola oil

1/2 cup lime juice

1/2 cup thinly sliced red onion

12 lemon slices

1 tablespoon minced fresh parsley

1/2 teaspoon salt

1/2 teaspoon dill weed

1/8 teaspoon hot pepper sauce

2 pounds medium shrimp, cooked, peeled and deveined

> In a large bowl, combine the first eight ingredients. Stir in shrimp. Cover and refrigerate for 4 hours, stirring occasionally. Drain the marinade before serving.

FESTIVE STUFFED DATES

PREP: 15 MIN. + CHILLING YIELD: 10 SERVINGS

DIANA DEBRUYN CINCINNATI, OH

Four ingredients are all you need to make these sweet and satisfying change-of-pace treats.

3 ounces reduced-fat cream cheese

1/4 cup confectioners' sugar

2 teaspoons grated orange peel

30 pitted dates

> In a small bowl, beat cream cheese, confectioners' sugar and grated orange peel until well blended.

> Carefully make a slit in the center of each date; fill with cream cheese mixture. Cover and refrigerate for at least 1 hour before serving.

SMOKED SALMON CHERRY TOMATOES

PREP/TOTAL TIME: 25 MIN. YIELD: 2-1/2 DOZEN

PAT CRONIN LAREDO, TX

The bright red bites are a showstopping finger food. With a smoked salmon filling, the stuffed tomatoes have restaurant-quality flair but are easy enough to make at home.

30 cherry tomatoes

3 ounces smoked salmon or lox, finely chopped

1/3 cup finely chopped onion

1/3 cup finely chopped green pepper

Salt and pepper to taste

1 package (3 ounces) cream cheese, softened

1 teaspoon milk

Fresh dill sprigs

> Cut a thin slice off each tomato top; scoop out and discard pulp. Invert tomatoes on paper towels to drain. In a large bowl, combine the salmon, onion, green pepper, salt and pepper. Spoon into tomatoes.

> In a small bowl, beat cream cheese and milk until smooth. Insert a star tip into a pastry or plastic bag. Pipe a small amount of cream cheese mixture onto tomatoes. Garnish with dill.

REBECCA ROSE
MT. WASHINGTON, KY

This is one of my favorite starters. We have a lot of pig roasts here in Kentucky, and these small sandwiches are perfect to serve while the pig roasts.

CUCUMBER PARTY SANDWICHES

PREP: 20 MIN. + STANDING YIELD: 2-1/2 DOZEN

1 package (8 ounces) cream cheese, softened

2 tablespoons mayonnaise

2 teaspoons Italian salad dressing mix

30 slices snack rye bread

30 thin slices cucumber

Fresh dill sprigs and chive blossoms

> In a large bowl, beat the cream cheese, mayonnaise and dressing mix until blended. Let stand for 30 minutes.

> Spread cream cheese on rye bread. Top each with a slice of cucumber, dill sprig and chive blossom. Cover and refrigerate until serving.

tips&ideas

Chive blossoms are the pretty, purple-pink flowers on the tips of the chive stems. Not only do the blossoms add a burst of fresh color to recipes, they also lend a slight peppery flavor. If you do not have access to fresh chives and chive blossoms in your own garden, pay a visit your local farmers market.

MARIE HATTRUP
THE DALLES, OR

The tart cranberry flavor blends nicely with the mustard and horseradish in this unique cracker-and-spread starter.

ZIPPY CRANBERRY APPETIZER

PREP: 20 MIN. + CHILLING YIELD: 2-1/2 CUPS

1/2 cup sugar

1/2 cup packed brown sugar

1 cup water

1 package (12 ounces) fresh or frozen cranberries

1 to 3 tablespoons prepared horseradish

1 tablespoon Dijon mustard

1 package (8 ounces) cream cheese, softened

Assorted crackers

> In a large saucepan, bring sugars and water to a boil over medium heat. Stir in cranberries; return to a boil. Cook for 10 minutes or until thickened, stirring occasionally. Cool.

> Stir in horseradish and mustard. Transfer to a large bowl; refrigerate until chilled. Just before serving, spread cream cheese over crackers; top with cranberry mixture.

tips&ideas

Fresh cranberries are in season from early fall through December. This is a great time to stock up on the tart berries for use in recipes throughout the year. Look for shiny, bright red berries. To freeze, place them in a single layer on a 13-inch x 9-inch baking pan. When frozen, transfer to an airtight container and freeze for up to 1 year.

JALAPENOS WITH OLIVE-CREAM FILLING

PREP/TOTAL TIME: 25 MIN. YIELD: 32 APPETIZERS

KRISTAL PETERSON WALKER, LA

These jalapenos are great! I take the spicy, stuffed bites to all get-togethers and potlucks, and the people at my husband's work are always requesting them.

1 package (8 ounces) cream cheese, softened

1/4 cup chopped pimiento-stuffed olives

2 tablespoons olive juice

16 large jalapeno peppers, halved lengthwise and seeded

> In a small bowl, combine the cream cheese, olives and olive juice. Spoon about 2 teaspoons into each jalapeno half. Serve stuffed jalapenos immediately or refrigerate until serving.

Editor's Note: When cutting hot peppers, disposable gloves are recommended. Avoid touching your face.

ANTIPASTO KABOBS

PREP: 35 MIN. + MARINATING YIELD: 40 APPETIZERS

DENISE HAZEN CINCINNATI, OH

My husband and I met at a cooking class and have loved creating menus and entertaining ever since. These do-ahead appetizers are always a hit and one of our favorites.

1 package (9 ounces) refrigerated cheese tortellini

40 pimiento-stuffed olives

40 large pitted ripe olives

3/4 cup Italian salad dressing

40 thin slices pepperoni

20 thin slices hard salami, halved

Fresh parsley sprigs, optional

> Cook tortellini according to package directions; drain and rinse in cold water. In a large resealable plastic bag, combine the tortellini, olives and salad dressing. Seal bag and turn to coat; refrigerate for 4 hours or overnight.

> Drain and discard marinade. For each appetizer, thread a stuffed olive, folded pepperoni slice, tortellini, folded salami piece, ripe olive and parsley sprig if desired on a toothpick or short skewer.

tips&ideas

When a recipe calls for chopped olives, do so quickly, easily and without a mess. Simply open the jar and drain the liquid. Then carefully move a sharp knife up and down and back and forth in the jar to chop the olives.

grits 'n' shrimp tarts, p. 83

Cute, dainty and simply irresistible, these handheld nibbles add elegance and variety to your appetizer offerings. Darling crostini, canapes, tarts and more await.

grab&go

MINI BURGERS
WITH THE WORKS

PREP/TOTAL TIME: 30 MIN. YIELD: 1 DOZEN

LINDA LANE BENNINGTON, VT

I started preparing these mini burgers several years ago as a way to use up bread crusts accumulating in my freezer. They're delicious, hearty and disappear fast.

1/4 pound ground beef

3 slices process American cheese

4 slices white bread (heels of loaf recommended)

2 tablespoons prepared Thousand Island salad dressing

2 pearl onions, thinly sliced

4 baby dill pickles, thinly sliced

3 cherry tomatoes, thinly sliced

> Shape beef into twelve 1-in. patties. Place on a microwave-safe plate lined with paper towels. Cover with another paper towel; microwave on high for 1 minute or until meat is no longer pink. Cut each slice of cheese into fourths; set aside.

> Using a 1-in. round cookie cutter, cut out six circles from each slice of bread. Spread half of the bread circles with dressing. Layer with the burgers, cheese, onions, pickles and tomatoes. Top with remaining bread circles; secure with toothpicks. Serve immediately.

Editor's Note: This recipe was tested in a 1,100-watt microwave.

MOZZARELLA
TOMATO TARTLETS

PREP/TOTAL TIME: 20 MIN. YIELD: 2 DOZEN

AMY GOLDEN EAST AURORA, NY

Convenient frozen phyllo shells contribute to this impressive appetizer's easy preparation. Although I make them year-round, they're especially tasty with garden-fresh tomatoes.

1 garlic clove, minced

1 tablespoon olive oil

1-1/2 cups seeded chopped tomatoes

3/4 cup shredded part-skim mozzarella cheese

1/2 teaspoon dried basil

Pepper to taste

24 frozen miniature phyllo tart shells

6 pitted ripe olives, quartered

Grated Parmesan cheese

> In a small skillet, saute garlic in oil for 1 minute. Add the tomatoes; cook until liquid has evaporated. Remove from the heat; stir in the mozzarella cheese, basil and pepper.

> Spoon 1 teaspoonful into each tart shell. Top each with an olive piece; sprinkle with Parmesan cheese. Place on an ungreased baking sheet. Bake at 450° for 5-8 minutes or until bubbly.

JERRI PEACHEE
GENTRY, AR

Packed with zippy Cajun flavor, these handheld morsels start with refrigerated buttermilk biscuits. A blend of pork sausage, cheese, green peppers and seasonings makes it hard to eat just one.

CAJUN CANAPES

PREP: 40 MIN. BAKE: 10 MIN. YIELD: 20 APPETIZERS

2 tubes (12 ounces each) refrigerated buttermilk biscuits

1/2 pound bulk pork sausage, cooked and drained

1-1/2 cups (6 ounces) shredded cheddar cheese

1/4 cup chopped green pepper

1/4 cup mayonnaise

2 green onions, chopped

2 teaspoons lemon juice

1/2 teaspoon salt

1/2 teaspoon paprika

1/4 teaspoon garlic powder

1/4 teaspoon dried thyme

1/8 to 1/4 teaspoon cayenne pepper

> Bake biscuits according to package directions, except turn biscuits over halfway through baking. Remove from pans to wire racks to cool completely.

> Using a melon baller, scoop out center of each biscuit, leaving a 3/8-in. shell (discard biscuit center or save for another use). In a small bowl, combine remaining ingredients. Spoon about 1 tablespoonful into the center of each biscuit.

> Place on an ungreased baking sheet. Bake at 400° for 8-10 minutes or until heated through. Serve warm.

tips&ideas

If you chopped more green onions than you need in your recipe, store the leftovers in a covered, clean glass jar in the refrigerator. They'll last a couple of weeks this way.

JANETTE ROOT
ELLENSBURG, WA

Whenever the ladies of our church host a bridal shower, these pita sandwiches appear on the menu. Not only are they simple and flavorful, they look nice on the table.

PARTY PITAS

PREP/TOTAL TIME: 15 MIN. YIELD: 32 SANDWICH WEDGES

1 package (8 ounces) cream cheese, softened

1/2 cup mayonnaise

1/2 teaspoon dill weed

1/4 teaspoon garlic salt

8 miniature pita pockets

16 fresh spinach leaves

3/4 pound shaved fully cooked ham

1/2 pound thinly sliced Monterey Jack cheese

> In a small bowl, beat the cream cheese, mayonnaise, dill and garlic salt until blended.

> Cut each pita in half horizontally; spread 1 tablespoon cream cheese mixture on each cut surface. On eight pita halves, layer the spinach, ham and cheese. Top with remaining pita halves. Cut each pita into four wedges; secure with toothpicks.

tips&ideas

When transporting food to an event, take two coolers—one for hot food and one for cold items. You'll be amazed at how well the coolers keep your contributions at their appropriate temperatures.

MINI SPINACH FRITTATAS

PREP/TOTAL TIME: 30 MIN. YIELD: 2 DOZEN

NANCY STATKEVICUS TUCSON, AZ

These mini frittatas are always a cinch to make and just delectable. The recipe doubles easily for a crowd and even freezes well for added convenience.

1 cup ricotta cheese

3/4 cup grated Parmesan cheese

2/3 cup chopped fresh mushrooms

1 package (10 ounces) frozen chopped spinach, thawed and squeezed dry

1 egg

1/2 teaspoon dried oregano

1/4 teaspoon salt

1/4 teaspoon pepper

24 slices pepperoni

> In a small bowl, combine the first eight ingredients. Place a slice of pepperoni in each of 24 greased miniature muffin cups. Fill muffin cups three-fourths full with cheese mixture.

> Bake at 375° for 20-25 minutes or until a toothpick comes out clean. Carefully run a knife around edges of muffin cups to loosen. Serve warm.

ARTICHOKE VEGGIE PIZZA

PREP: 40 MIN. BAKE: 15 MIN. + CHILLING YIELD: 3 DOZEN.

TASTE OF HOME TEST KITCHEN GREENDALE, WI

Our home economists used sun-dried tomato spread as the base for this vegetable-laden appetizer. Its garden-fresh taste and colorful appearance will make it one of the first items to disappear from any buffet.

1 tube (13.8 ounces) refrigerated pizza crust

1 package (8 ounces) cream cheese, softened

1/2 cup sun-dried tomato spread

1 can (14 ounces) water-packed artichoke hearts, rinsed, drained and finely chopped

1/2 cup chopped sweet onion

1 can (4-1/4 ounces) chopped ripe olives, drained

3/4 cup sliced carrots

3/4 cup chopped green pepper

1-1/2 cups fresh broccoli florets, chopped

1 cup (4 ounces) shredded Italian cheese blend

> Press pizza dough into a greased 15-in. x 10-in. baking pan. Prick dough thoroughly with a fork. Bake at 400° for 13-15 minutes or until golden brown. Cool.

> In a small bowl, beat cream cheese and tomato spread until blended. Stir in artichokes. Spread over crust. Sprinkle with the onion, olives, carrots, green pepper, broccoli and cheese; press down lightly. Chill for 1 hour. Cut into squares. Refrigerate leftovers.

PEPPERED CHICKEN PIZZA

PREP: 55 MIN. + RISING BAKE: 15 MIN.
YIELD: 20 APPETIZER SERVINGS

JULIE DERUWE OAKVILLE, WA

A homemade crust is topped with tender chicken, barbecue sauce, red pepper flakes and broiled peppers in this crowd-pleasing specialty. I like to prepare the vegetables and other toppings in advance so I can assemble this pizza quickly.

2 packages (1/4 ounce each) active dry yeast

1 cup warm water (110° to 115°)

2 cups bread flour

1 cup all-purpose flour

2 tablespoons olive oil

2 teaspoons sugar

1 teaspoon salt

TOPPING:

2 tablespoons olive oil

3 garlic cloves, minced

3/4 teaspoon salt

1 each medium green, sweet red and yellow pepper, julienned

1/2 medium red onion, sliced and separated into rings

1/2 pound boneless skinless chicken breast, cut into 1/4-inch strips

1/4 teaspoon crushed red pepper flakes

2/3 cup hickory smoke-flavored barbecue sauce

1-1/2 cups (6 ounces) shredded part-skim mozzarella cheese

1-1/2 cups (6 ounces) shredded reduced-fat Mexican cheese blend

> In a large bowl, dissolve yeast in warm water. Stir in the flours, oil, sugar and salt until smooth. Turn onto a lightly floured surface; knead until smooth and elastic, about 6 minutes. Place in a bowl coated with cooking spray, turning once to coat top. Cover and let rise in a warm place until doubled, about 45 minutes.

> Punch down dough; let stand for 10 minutes. Roll out to a 15-in. x 10-in. rectangle. Place in a 15-in. x 10-in. pan coated with cooking spray. Let dough stand for 10 minutes. Prick dough with a fork. Bake at 375° for 7 minutes.

> Meanwhile, in a small bowl, combine the oil, garlic and salt; let stand for 15 minutes. Place peppers and onion on a baking sheet; drizzle with half of the oil mixture. Broil 4 in. from the heat for 5 minutes or until vegetables are tender and lightly browned; set aside.

> Toss chicken with pepper flakes and remaining oil mixture; place on a baking sheet. Broil 4 in. from the heat for 5 minutes or until chicken juices run clear.

> Arrange the vegetables and chicken strips over crust. Drizzle with barbecue sauce; sprinkle with cheeses. Bake pizza for 15-20 minutes or until lightly browned.

BRIE PHYLLO CUPS

PREP/TOTAL TIME: 20 MIN. YIELD: 15 APPETIZERS

BRENDA LITTLE BOISE, ID

Mini phyllo shells from the freezer section hurry along these elegant cups. The creamy bites look fancy and taste divine but are a snap to put together for a special occasion.

1 package (1.9 ounces) frozen miniature phyllo tart shells

3 tablespoons crushed gingersnaps

6 ounces Brie or Camembert cheese, rind removed, cubed

1/4 cup spreadable fruit of your choice

> Place the tart shells on an ungreased baking sheet. Sprinkle about 1/2 teaspoon gingersnap crumbs into each shell; top with Brie and the spreadable fruit. Bake at 325° for 5 minutes or until cheese is melted.

TASTE OF HOME
TEST KITCHEN
GREENDALE, WI

*A creamy, homemade
cucumber yogurt
sauce complements
tender slices of beef
in this recipe from
our Test Kitchen.*

BEEF CANAPES WITH CUCUMBER SAUCE

PREP: 30 MIN. + CHILLING BAKE: 25 MIN. + CHILLING YIELD: 3 DOZEN

4 cups (32 ounces) plain yogurt

1 whole beef tenderloin
(1-1/2 pounds)

2 tablespoons olive oil, divided

1 teaspoon salt, divided

1/4 teaspoon plus 1/8 teaspoon
white pepper, divided

1 medium cucumber, peeled,
seeded and diced

1 tablespoon finely chopped onion

1 garlic clove, minced

1 tablespoon white vinegar

1 French bread baguette (1 pound),
cut into 36 thin slices

1 cup fresh arugula

Sliced grape tomatoes, optional

> Line a fine mesh strainer with two layers of cheesecloth; place over a bowl. Place yogurt in strainer. Cover and refrigerate for at least 4 hours or overnight.

> Rub tenderloin with 1 tablespoon oil. Sprinkle with 1/2 teaspoon salt and 1/4 teaspoon white pepper. In a large skillet, cook tenderloin over medium-high heat until browned on all sides. Transfer to a shallow roasting pan.

> Bake at 400° for 25-30 minutes or until a meat thermometer reads 145°. Cool on a wire rack for 1 hour. Cover and refrigerate.

> Transfer yogurt from strainer to another bowl (discard yogurt liquid). Add the cucumber, onion, garlic and remaining salt and white pepper. In a small bowl, whisk the vinegar and remaining oil; stir into yogurt mixture.

> Thinly slice the tenderloin. Spread yogurt mixture over bread slices; top with beef, arugula and tomato slices if desired. Serve immediately or cover and refrigerate until serving.

HEIDI MELLON
WAUKESHA, WI

After I'd tasted this quick, yummy pizza at a party, I knew I had to have the recipe. I've been serving it for many years, and it still disappears in minutes.

CRANBERRY CAMEMBERT PIZZA

PREP: 15 MIN. BAKE: 20 MIN. YIELD: 12-14 APPETIZER SLICES

1 tube (13.8 ounces) refrigerated pizza crust

8 ounces Camembert or Brie cheese, rind removed and cut into 1/2-inch cubes

3/4 cup whole-berry cranberry sauce

1/2 cup chopped pecans

> Unroll crust onto a lightly greased 12-in. pizza pan; flatten dough and build up edges slightly. Bake at 425° for 10-12 minutes or until crust is light golden brown.

> Sprinkle cheese over crust. Spoon cranberry sauce evenly over crust; sprinkle with pecans.

> Bake 8-10 minutes longer or until cheese is melted and crust is golden brown. Cool for 5 minutes before cutting.

GRILLED FETA QUESADILLAS

PREP/TOTAL TIME: 20 MIN. YIELD: 12 WEDGES

JACQUI CORREA LANDING, NJ

*This appetizer is a favorite whenever we have company,
I had something similar at a Memorial Day party and I tried
to re-create the flavor using lower-fat ingredients. No one even
notices that these tangy bites are good for you!*

3 ounces fat-free cream cheese

1/2 cup shredded reduced-fat Mexican cheese blend

1/3 cup crumbled feta cheese

1/2 teaspoon dried oregano

4 flour tortillas (6 inches)

1/4 cup chopped pitted ripe olives

2 tablespoons diced pimientos

1 green onion, chopped

> In a small bowl, beat cheeses with oregano until
blended. Spread 3 tablespoons of cheese mixture
over half of each tortilla; top with olives,
pimientos and onion. Fold tortillas over.

> Coat grill rack with cooking spray before starting
the grill. Grill quesadillas, uncovered, over
medium heat for 1-2 minutes on each side or until
golden brown. Cut each quesadilla into three
wedges. Serve warm.

GUACAMOLE APPETIZER SQUARES

PREP: 20 MIN. BAKE: 10 MIN. + COOLING
YIELD: ABOUT 3 DOZEN

LAURIE PESTER COLSTRIP, MT

*This cold appetizer pizza has appeared at family functions for
many years. People rave about its Southwestern flavor.*

2 tubes (8 ounces each) refrigerated crescent rolls

1-1/2 teaspoons taco seasoning

1 package (1 pound) sliced bacon, diced

1 package (8 ounces) cream cheese, softened

1-1/2 cups guacamole

3 plum tomatoes, chopped

1 can (3.8 ounces) sliced ripe olives, drained

> Unroll both tubes of crescent dough and pat into
an ungreased 15-in. x 10-in. baking pan; seal
seams and perforations. Build up edges. Prick
dough with a fork; sprinkle with taco seasoning.
Bake at 375° for 10-12 minutes or until golden
brown. Cool completely on a wire rack.

> In a large skillet, cook bacon over medium heat
until crisp. Using a slotted spoon, remove to
paper towels. In a small bowl, beat cream cheese
and guacamole until smooth.

> Spread cream cheese mixture over crust. Sprinkle
with bacon, tomatoes and olives. Refrigerate until
serving. Cut into squares.

reaches desired doneness (for medium-rare, a meat thermometer should read 145°; medium, 160°; well-done, 170°). Let stand for 10 minutes.

> In a small bowl, beat horseradish and remaining butter until blended. Spread over bread slices. Place on a baking sheet. Broil 3-4 in. from heat for 2-3 minutes or until lightly golden brown. Thinly slice the beef; place on toasted bread. Top with caramelized onions. Garnish with parsley.

APPLE-GOAT CHEESE BRUSCHETTA

PREP/TOTAL TIME: 20 MIN. YIELD: 16 APPETIZERS

LAURA PERRY CHESTER SPRINGS, PA

It takes just six ingredients and 20 minutes to put together this eye-catching bruschetta. Crunchy apple and warm goat cheese top these crispy treats to create a fantastic flavor combination.

16 slices French bread (1/2 inch thick)

1 medium Fuji apple, chopped

1/4 cup crumbled goat cheese

3/4 teaspoon minced fresh thyme

1/2 teaspoon minced fresh oregano

1/4 teaspoon coarsely ground pepper

> Place bread slices on an ungreased baking sheet. Broil 3-4 in. from the heat for 1-2 minutes or until golden brown. Combine the apple, goat cheese, thyme, oregano and pepper; sprinkle over bread. Broil 1 minute longer or until cheese is softened.

PEPPER-CRUSTED TENDERLOIN CROSTINI

PREP: 45 MIN. BAKE: 20 MIN. + STANDING YIELD: 2-1/2 DOZEN

TASTE OF HOME TEST KITCHEN GREENDALE, WI

Caramelized onions add a touch of sweetness to this elegant appetizer developed by our home economists. Use the higher range of pepper if you like a little more zip.

2 large onions, thinly sliced

6 tablespoons butter, softened, divided

2 teaspoons sugar

1 tablespoon olive oil

1 beef tenderloin (1-1/2 pounds)

2 to 3 teaspoons coarsely ground pepper

2 garlic cloves, minced

3/4 teaspoon salt

2 teaspoons prepared horseradish

1 French bread baguette (10-1/2 ounces), cut into 30 slices

Minced fresh parsley

> In a large skillet over medium-low heat, cook onions in 3 tablespoons butter for 5 minutes or until tender. Add sugar; cook over low heat for 30-40 minutes longer or until onions are golden brown, stirring frequently.

> Meanwhile, rub oil over tenderloin. Combine the pepper, garlic and salt; rub over beef. In a large skillet, brown beef on all sides. Transfer to a baking sheet. Bake at 425° for 20-25 minutes or until meat

ELIZABETH LATADY
JACKSON, MS

This cute, deliciously different appetizer showcases two Mississippi staples— grits and shrimp. I know your family will enjoy them as much as mine!

GRITS 'N' SHRIMP TARTS

PREP/TOTAL TIME: 30 MIN. YIELD: 2-1/2 DOZEN

1 cup water

1/4 cup quick-cooking grits

2 ounces cream cheese, softened

1/4 cup shredded cheddar cheese

3 tablespoons butter, divided

1/4 teaspoon garlic salt

1/8 teaspoon salt

Pepper to taste

1 pound uncooked small shrimp, peeled and deveined

3 green onions, sliced

2 packages (1.9 ounces each) frozen miniature phyllo tart shells

> In a small saucepan, bring water to a boil. Gradually stir in grits. Reduce heat; cover and simmer for 4 minutes. Stir in the cheeses, 1 tablespoon butter, garlic salt, salt and pepper.

> In a large skillet, saute shrimp and onions in remaining butter until shrimp turn pink. Fill tart shells with grits; top with shrimp mixture. Refrigerate leftovers.

tips&ideas

Phyllo (pronounced FEE-lo) is a tissue-thin dough generally sold in the freezer section of grocery stores. Phyllo dough is liberally basted with melted butter between each sheet so that it bakes up crisp and flaky. It's used for desserts, appetizers and savory main dishes.

MARIAN PLATT
SEQUIM, WA

For a picnic, I whisked this tart out of the oven, wrapped it in foil and headed out the door. My friends were surprised and delighted when they tasted it.

ROASTED PEPPER TART

PREP: 20 MIN. + CHILLING BAKE: 40 MIN. + COOLING YIELD: 12 SERVINGS

1-1/2 cups all-purpose flour

1/8 teaspoon salt

1/2 cup cold butter

3 to 4 tablespoons water

3 medium sweet red peppers, halved and seeded

2 medium green bell peppers, halved and seeded

1/3 cup olive oil

2 garlic cloves, minced

4-1/2 teaspoons minced fresh oregano

2 cups (8 ounces) shredded Monterey Jack cheese, divided

1 can (2-1/4 ounces) sliced ripe olives, drained

> In a large bowl, combine flour and salt; cut in butter until crumbly. Gradually add water, tossing with a fork until dough forms a ball. Cover and refrigerate for 1 hour.

> Broil peppers 4 in. from the heat until skins are blistered and blackened, about 10 minutes. Immediately place peppers in a bowl; cover and let stand for 15-20 minutes. Peel off and discard charred skin. Coarsely chop peppers; place in a bowl. Add oil, garlic and oregano; toss to coat. Set aside.

> Roll out dough to fit a 12-in. pizza pan. Transfer to pan. Prick dough thoroughly with a fork. Bake at 350° for 30-35 minutes or until lightly browned and crust begins pulling away from edges of pan. Let crust cool completely.

> Sprinkle 1 cup cheese over crust. Sprinkle with pepper mixture and remaining cheese. Arrange olives around edge. Bake at 350° for 10-15 minutes or until cheese is melted. Serve immediately.

BERRY BRUSCHETTA

PREP/TOTAL TIME: 20 MIN. YIELD: 32 APPETIZERS

TASTE OF HOME TEST KITCHEN GREENDALE, WI
Our Test Kitchen is the source of this fantastic, fruity bruschetta. It's a tasty twist from the traditional tomato variety and can be served as an appetizer or dessert.

1 French bread baguette (1 pound)

2 tablespoons olive oil

1-1/2 cups chopped fresh strawberries

3/4 cup chopped peeled fresh peaches

1-1/2 teaspoons minced fresh mint

1/2 cup Mascarpone cheese

> Cut baguette into 32 slices, about 1/2 in. thick; place on ungreased baking sheets. Brush with oil. Broil 6-8 in. from the heat for 1-2 minutes or until lightly toasted.

> In a small bowl, combine the strawberries, peaches and mint. Spread each slice of bread with Mascarpone cheese; top with fruit mixture. Broil for 1-2 minutes or until cheese is slightly melted. Serve immediately.

HAM 'N' CHEESE BISCUIT STACKS

PREP: 1 HOUR BAKE: 10 MIN. + COOLING YIELD: 40 APPETIZERS

KELLY WILLIAMS LAPORTE, IN
I make these finger sandwiches for holidays and Super Bowl parties, too. They're pretty enough for a baby shower and hearty enough for the guys.

2 tubes (12 ounces each) refrigerated buttermilk biscuits

3/4 cup stone-ground mustard, divided

1/2 cup butter, softened

1/4 cup chopped green onions

1/4 cup mayonnaise

1/4 cup honey

10 thick slices deli ham

10 slices Swiss cheese

2-1/2 cups shredded romaine

40 frilled toothpicks

20 pitted ripe olives, drained and patted dry

20 pimiento-stuffed olives, drained and patted dry

> Cut each biscuit in half, forming half circles. Place 2 in. apart on ungreased baking sheets. Spread each with 1/2 teaspoon mustard. Bake at 400° for 8-10 minutes or until golden brown. Remove from pans to wire racks to cool.

> In a small bowl, combine the butter and onions. In another bowl, combine the mayonnaise, honey and remaining mustard. Cut each slice of ham into four rectangles; cut each slice of cheese into four triangles.

> Split each biscuit in half; spread bottom halves with butter mixture. Layer one ham piece, one cheese piece and 1 tablespoon romaine on each biscuit bottom. Spread mustard mixture over biscuit tops; place over romaine. Thread toothpicks through olives; insert into stacks. Refrigerate leftovers.

mulled grape cider, p. 91

From **rich, decadent** dessert drinks and soothing cappucinos to classic cocktails and **sparkling** punches... delight in the simple **pleasures** poured into every cup.

coffee & beverages

COCOA FOR A CROWD
PREP/TOTAL TIME: 15 MIN. YIELD: 65 (1-CUP) SERVINGS

JULIA LIVINGSTON FROSTPROOF, FL
You will warm many hearts with this rich, satisfying cocoa. It is the perfect beverage to serve after an ice-skating outing or any cold winter gathering.

5 cups baking cocoa

3 cups sugar

2 teaspoons salt

5 quarts water, divided

10 quarts milk

1 quart heavy whipping cream

2 tablespoons vanilla extract

Whipped cream and additional baking cocoa

> In each of two large stockpots, combine 2-1/2 cups cocoa, 1-1/2 cups sugar and 1 teaspoon salt. Gradually stir 5 cups water into each pot. Bring to a boil; reduce heat. Whisk in the milk, cream and remaining water; heat through. Remove from the heat; stir in vanilla. Garnish with whipped cream and additional cocoa.

MULLED MERLOT
PREP: 10 MIN. COOK: 1 HOUR YIELD: 9 SERVINGS

TASTE OF HOME TEST KITCHEN GREENDALE, WI
Our home economists created this classy beverage recipe that's sure to warm up your party guests!

4 cinnamon sticks (3 inches)

4 whole cloves

2 bottles (750 milliliters each) merlot

1/2 cup sugar

1/2 cup orange juice

1/2 cup brandy

1 medium orange, thinly sliced

> Place cinnamon sticks and cloves on a double thickness of cheesecloth; bring up corners of cloth and tie with string to form a bag.

> In a 3-qt. slow cooker, combine the wine, sugar, orange juice, brandy and orange slices. Add spice bag. Cover and cook on high for 1 hour or until heated through. Discard spice bag and orange slices. Serve warm in mugs.

PAULA ZSIRAY
LOGAN, UT

This recipe's name says it all. With very little effort, you can still enjoy the delicious traditional flavor of eggnog...and without using any eggs!

EFFORTLESS EGGNOG

PREP/TOTAL TIME: 5 MIN. YIELD: 16 SERVINGS (2 QUARTS)

1/2 gallon cold milk, divided

1 package (3.4 ounces) instant French vanilla pudding mix

1/4 cup sugar

2 teaspoons vanilla extract

1/2 teaspoon ground cinnamon

1/2 teaspoon ground nutmeg

> In a large bowl, whisk 3/4 cup milk and pudding mix until smooth. Whisk in the sugar, vanilla, cinnamon and nutmeg. Stir in the remaining milk. Refrigerate until serving.

tips&ideas

Garnish coffee drinks, desserts and cakes with a few sprinkles of baking cocoa or instant chocolate drink mix for an enticing, pretty look. Use a shaker—like the ones that hold powdered sugar—for speedy sifting over coffee, pastries and even desserts.

JUDIE WHITE
FLORIEN, LA

You can stir up this punch without a fuss because it calls for only a few ingredients. The pretty cranberry ice ring adds festive flair.

CRIMSON CRANBERRY PUNCH

PREP: 20 MIN. + FREEZING YIELD: 5 QUARTS

1/2 cup frozen cranberries

3-1/2 cups cold water

1 bottle (48 ounces) white grape juice, chilled

2 cans (12 ounces each) frozen cranberry juice concentrate, thawed

4 cans (12 ounces each) diet lemon-lime soda, chilled

3 orange slices

3 lemon slices

> Place the cranberries in a 4-1/2-cup ring mold coated with cooking spray. Slowly pour a small amount of cold water into the mold to barely cover berries; freeze until solid. Add remaining water; freeze until ring is solid.

> Just before serving, combine the grape juice and cranberry juice concentrate in a large punch bowl; stir in soda. Unmold ice ring; place fruit side up in punch bowl. Add orange and lemon slices.

tips&ideas

Unmolding an ice ring is easier than you might think. To remove an ice ring from a mold, wrap the bottom of the mold with a hot, damp dish towel. Invert the mold onto a baking sheet and place the ice ring fruit side up in the punch bowl.

MULLED GRAPE CIDER

PREP: 20 MIN. COOK: 3 HOURS
YIELD: 10-12 SERVINGS (2-3/4 QUARTS)

SHARON HARMON ORANGE, MA
Here's a soothing change of pace from traditional apple cider. A warm mug of this grape-flavored beverage serves up comfort in every single sip.

5 pounds Concord grapes

8 cups water, divided

1-1/2 cups sugar

8 whole cloves

4 cinnamon sticks (4 inches)

Dash ground nutmeg

> In a large saucepan or Dutch oven, combine grapes and 2 cups water; bring to a boil, stirring constantly. Press through a strainer; reserve juice and discard skins and seeds.

> Pour juice through a double layer of cheesecloth into a 5-qt. slow cooker. Add the sugar, cloves, cinnamon sticks, nutmeg and remaining water. Cover and cook on low for 3 hours. Discard cloves and cinnamon sticks.

WISCONSIN BRANDY OLD-FASHIONED SWEET

PREP/TOTAL TIME: 10 MIN. YIELD: 1 SERVING

TASTE OF HOME TEST KITCHEN GREENDALE, WI
The concept of an old-fashioned dates back to the early 1800s and includes whiskey, bitters, cherry juice, sugar and water. This version, created by our home economists, is extremely popular in Wisconsin. It uses brandy in place of whiskey and lemon-lime soda instead of water for a milder tasting cocktail.

1 orange slice

1 maraschino cherry

1-1/2 ounces maraschino cherry juice

1 teaspoon bitters

1/4 to 1/3 cup ice cubes

1-1/2 ounces brandy

2 teaspoons water

1 teaspoon orange juice

3 ounces lemon-lime soda

> In a rocks glass, muddle the orange slice, cherry, cherry juice and bitters. Add ice. Pour in the brandy, water, orange juice and soda.

TOFFEE-FLAVORED COFFEE

PREP/TOTAL TIME: 15 MIN. YIELD: 5 SERVINGS

TASTE OF HOME TEST KITCHEN GREENDALE, WI
With its chocolate-toffee flavor, this rich java drink from our home economists makes mornings pleasant. Treat yourself to a cup in the afternoon as a special pick-me-up, too.

1/2 cup heavy whipping cream

1 tablespoon confectioners' sugar

1/2 cup milk chocolate toffee bits

5 cups hot brewed coffee

2 tablespoons butterscotch ice cream topping

> In a small bowl, beat cream until it begins to thicken. Add confectioners' sugar; beat until stiff peaks form. Stir toffee bits into coffee; let stand for 30 seconds. Strain and discard any undissolved toffee bits. Pour coffee into mugs; top with whipped cream and drizzle with butterscotch topping.

EGGNOG COFFEE

PREP/TOTAL TIME: 10 MIN. YIELD: 4 SERVINGS

TASTE OF HOME TEST KITCHEN GREENDALE, WI
A classic Christmas drink gets a coffee kick in this luscious creation. Just two ingredients make this soothing beverage.

1-1/3 cups eggnog

2-2/3 cups hot strong brewed coffee
(French or other dark roast)

Whipped cream and ground nutmeg,
optional

> Place eggnog in a large saucepan. Cook and stir until heated through. (Do not boil.) Stir in coffee. Pour into cups or mugs; serve immediately. Garnish coffee with whipped cream and ground nutmeg if desired.

Editor's Note: This recipe was tested with commercially prepared eggnog.

tips&ideas

Chocolate-covered spoons make delicious stirrers for hot beverages—and look lovely, too. To make them, melt chocolate or vanilla chips and shortening in a microwave-safe bowl. Once melted, coat the spoons and sprinkle with coarse sugar, jimmies or crushed peppermint.

ELOISE NEELEY
NORTON, OH

As pretty as a fresh snowdrift, this frothy, fruity punch has been a Christmas tradition in our family for years. It is a refreshing thirst-quencher.

SNOW PUNCH

PREP/TOTAL TIME: 10 MIN. YIELD: 2-1/2 QUARTS

1 cup lemon juice

5 medium ripe bananas

1 cup sugar

2 cups half-and-half cream

1 liter lemon-lime soda, chilled

1 pint lemon or pineapple sherbet

1/4 cup flaked coconut, optional

> In a blender, cover and process the lemon juice, bananas and sugar until smooth. Add cream; blend until smooth. Cover and refrigerate.

> Just before serving, pour lemon-banana mixture into a punch bowl. Stir in soda. Top with sherbet and coconut if desired.

tips&ideas

Lemon spirals make an attractive garnish for Snow Punch. Use a citrus stripper to remove the peel of a lemon in one continuous motion, working from end to end. Tightly wind the strip around a straw, then trim and secure the ends with waterproof tape. Let stand for at least 20 minutes before unwinding the spirals from the straws.

TASTE OF HOME TEST KITCHEN
GREENDALE, WI

Five ingredients create this sweet sipper. Individual servings of the warm coffee creation are topped with whipped cream and whimsical butterscotch garnishes.

BUTTERSCOTCH COFFEE

PREP/TOTAL TIME: 20 MIN. YIELD: 8 SERVINGS (2 QUARTS)

1 cup butterscotch chips, divided

8 cups hot brewed coffee

1/2 cup half-and-half cream

5 to 8 tablespoons sugar

Whipped cream in a can

> In a small microwave-safe bowl, heat 1/2 cup butterscotch chips at 70% power until melted, stirring occasionally. Cut a small hole in the corner of a pastry or plastic bag; insert a #4 round tip. Fill bag with melted chips. Pipe eight garnishes onto a waxed paper-lined baking sheet. Refrigerate until set, about 10 minutes.

> In a large pitcher, stir coffee and remaining butterscotch chips until chips are melted. Stir in cream and sugar.

> Pour into mugs. Top each serving with whipped cream and a butterscotch garnish.

CITRUS WASSAIL

PREP/TOTAL TIME: 25 MIN.
YIELD: 13 SERVINGS (ABOUT 3 QUARTS)

JULIE WILLIQUETTE HARTSELLE, AL
I found this healthy wassail recipe in a cookbook. My daughter first prepared it to go with our day-after-Thanksgiving leftovers meal to everyone's enjoyment.

8 cups unsweetened apple juice

2 cups unsweetened pineapple juice

2 cups orange juice

1/2 cup lemon juice

1/4 cup sugar

1 teaspoon ground cinnamon

1/2 teaspoon ground cloves

> In a Dutch oven, combine all of the ingredients. Bring to a boil. Reduce heat; simmer, uncovered, for 10-15 minutes. Serve warm.

PEPPERMINT EGGNOG PUNCH

PREP/TOTAL TIME: 15 MIN. YIELD: 9 CUPS

MARJORIE JANE WATKINS EUGENE, OR
With peppermint ice cream and a candy cane garnish, this is almost more of a dessert than a beverage!

1 quart peppermint ice cream, softened

4 cups eggnog, chilled

1 cup rum or 2 teaspoons rum extract, optional

2 cups carbonated water, chilled

Miniature candy canes, optional

> Set aside a few scoops of ice cream to use as a garnish. Place the remaining ice cream in a large punch bowl; stir in the eggnog and rum or extract if desired. Add carbonated water. Top with reserved ice cream scoops. Serve with candy canes if desired. Serve immediately.

Editor's Note: This recipe was tested with commercially prepared eggnog.

WHITE RUSSIAN

PREP/TOTAL TIME: 5 MIN. YIELD: 1 SERVING

TASTE OF HOME TEST KITCHEN GREENDALE, WI
This indulgent, coffee-flavored drink is a star at any occasion and perfect for any season. It is equally appropriate to sip a glass before or after dinner.

1/2 to 3/4 cup ice cubes

1-1/2 ounces vodka

1-1/2 ounces Kahlua

3 ounces heavy whipping cream or milk

> Place ice in a rocks glass. Pour the vodka, Kahlua and cream into the glass.

FROSTY MOCHA DRINK

PREP/TOTAL TIME: 15 MIN. YIELD: 4 SERVINGS

LAUREN NANCE SAN DIEGO, CA
I make this chilly, chocolate-flavored coffee drink for special events. For a richer taste, replace milk with half-and-half cream.

1 cup milk

3 tablespoons instant chocolate drink mix

2 tablespoons instant coffee granules

2 tablespoons honey

1 teaspoon vanilla extract

14 to 16 ice cubes

> In a blender, combine all ingredients; cover and process until smooth. Pour into chilled glasses; serve immediately.

CHAMPAGNE PARTY PUNCH

PREP: 15 MIN. + CHILLING YIELD: 16-18 SERVINGS (3-1/2 QUARTS)

TASTE OF HOME TEST KITCHEN GREENDALE, WI
An assortment of juices, ginger ale and chilled champagne make this party punch a bubbly sensation. To make the presentation even more festive, float an ice ring in the punch.

1 cup sugar

1 cup water

2 cups unsweetened apple juice

2 cups unsweetened pineapple juice

1/2 cup lemon juice

1/3 cup frozen orange juice concentrate, thawed

1/4 cup lime juice

2 cups ice cubes

1 quart ginger ale, chilled

1 bottle (750 ml) Champagne, chilled

> In a large pitcher, combine the sugar and water; stir until sugar is dissolved. Add the apple juice, pineapple juice, lemon juice, orange juice concentrate and lime juice. Refrigerate until serving.

> Just before serving, pour into a punch bowl and add ice cubes. Slowly add ginger ale and Champagne.

tips&ideas

Jazz up your beverage glasses with garnished rims. Melt chocolate chips and shortening in a microwave-safe bowl, then dip the rims into the chocolate. Sprinkle baking cocoa or chocolate jimmies over the melted chocolate and let the glasses stand until the chocolate hardens.

ESTHER LAMBRIGHT
SHIPSHEWANA, IN

This hot chocolate mix features a tasty blend of mint and malt. We enjoy the rich treat each holiday season— especially after caroling!

MINTY HOT CHOCOLATE

PREP/TOTAL TIME: 15 MIN.   YIELD: 27 SERVINGS (6-3/4 CUPS MIX)

2 cups chocolate-flavored malted milk powder, divided

1 cup butter mints

3 cups nonfat dry milk powder

1-1/2 cups instant chocolate drink mix

EACH SERVING:

3/4 cup boiling water

Chocolate mint reception stick candies, optional

> In a food processor, combine 1 cup malted milk powder and mints; cover and process until smooth. Pour into a large bowl. Add milk powder, chocolate drink mix and remaining malted milk powder; mix well. Store in airtight containers.

> For each serving, combine 1/4 cup mix and 3/4 cup boiling water; stir until dissolved. Garnish with reception stick candies if desired.

tips&ideas

Chocolate curls are another yummy way to dress up cups of warm Minty Hot Chocolate. To make chocolate curls, use a vegetable peeler to peel off curls from a solid block of chocolate. Allow the curls to fall gently onto a work surface or plate in a single layer. If you get only shavings, try warming the chocolate slightly.

peanut butter mini muffins, p. 105

Charming bites and too-cute nibbles let you have your cake and eat it, too. Indulge your senses in this heavenly selection of mini muffins, pastries and tartlets.

sweet&decadent

WENDY NICKEL
KIESTER, MN

These delicious little bites have a surprise inside: a sweet raspberry jam filling. They're easy to make, fast to bake and taste oh-so good! My husband ate almost the entire batch of these yummy morsels.

RASPBERRY-CHOCOLATE MINI MUFFINS

PREP: 40 MIN. BAKE: 10 MIN. YIELD: 16 MUFFINS

2 tablespoons baking cocoa

1/4 cup boiling water

1/4 cup butter, softened

1/3 cup sugar

1 egg

2/3 cup all-purpose flour

1/2 teaspoon baking powder

4 teaspoons seedless raspberry jam

2 tablespoons chopped sliced almonds

1 teaspoon coarse sugar

> Dissolve cocoa in water; let stand until cool. Meanwhile, in a small bowl, cream butter and sugar until light and fluffy. Beat in egg. Combine flour and baking powder; add to creamed mixture alternately with cocoa mixture.

> Fill paper-lined miniature muffin cups half full. Drop 1/4 teaspoon of jam into the center of each; cover with 2 teaspoons batter. Sprinkle with almonds and sugar.

> Bake at 350° for 10-12 minutes or until a toothpick inserted in the chocolate portion comes out clean. Cool for 5 minutes before removing from pans to a wire rack. Serve warm.

STRAWBERRY TARTLETS

PREP: 25 MIN. BAKE: 10 MIN. + COOLING YIELD: 1 DOZEN

JOY VAN METER THORNTON, CO
This elegant-looking dessert is simple to prepare, and the cute wonton "cups" can be made in advance. They're a different way to present fresh strawberries when entertaining. The recipe is easy to double, too.

12 wonton wrappers

3 tablespoons butter, melted

1/3 cup packed brown sugar

3/4 cup Mascarpone cheese

2 tablespoons honey

2 teaspoons orange juice

3 cups fresh strawberries, sliced

Whipped cream and fresh mint, optional

> Brush one side of each wonton wrapper with butter. Place brown sugar in a shallow bowl; press buttered side of wontons into sugar to coat. Press wontons sugared side up into greased muffin cups.

> Bake at 325° for 7-9 minutes or until edges are lightly browned. Remove to a wire rack to cool.

> In a small bowl, combine the cheese, honey and orange juice. Spoon about 1 tablespoon into each wonton cup. Top with strawberries. Garnish with whipped cream and mint if desired.

WONTON KISSES

PREP/TOTAL TIME: 25 MIN. YIELD: 2 DOZEN

DARLENE BRENDEN SALEM, OR
These wrapped bundles filled with a sweet chocolate candy kiss are sure to delight guests at your next party.

24 milk chocolate kisses

24 wonton wrappers

Oil for frying

Confectioners' sugar

> Place a chocolate kiss in the center of a wonton wrapper. (Keep remaining wrappers covered with a damp paper towel until ready to use.) Moisten edges with water; fold opposite corners together over candy kiss and press to seal. Repeat.

> In an electric skillet, heat 1 in. of oil to 375°. Fry wontons for 2-1/2 minutes or until golden brown, turning once. Drain on paper towels. Dust with confectioners' sugar.

tips&ideas

The recipe for Wonton Kisses calls for an electric skillet for frying. If you don't have an electric fry pan with a thermostat, you can also use a kettle or Dutch oven together with a thermometer so you can accurately regulate the temperature of the oil.

more. Remove from the oven; add candy and mix well. Remove from pans and place on waxed paper to cool. Break into clusters. Store in airtight containers or plastic bags.

Editor's Note: We recommend that you test your candy thermometer before each use by bringing water to a boil; the thermometer should read 212°. Adjust your recipe temperature up or down based on your test.

BAKLAVA TARTLETS

PREP/TOTAL TIME: 25 MIN. YIELD: 45 TARTLETS

ASHLEY EAGON KETTERING, OH
Want a quick treat that's delicious and easy to do? These tartlets will do the trick. You can serve them right away, but they're better after chilling for about an hour in the refrigerator. A little sprig of mint adds a special touch.

2 cups finely chopped walnuts

3/4 cup honey

1/2 cup butter, melted

1 teaspoon ground cinnamon

1 teaspoon lemon juice

1/4 teaspoon ground cloves

3 packages (1.9 ounces each) frozen miniature phyllo tart shells

> In a small bowl, combine the first six ingredients; spoon 2 teaspoonfuls into each tart shell. Refrigerate until serving.

DELUXE CARAMEL CORN

PREP: 30 MIN. BAKE: 45 MIN. + COOLING YIELD: 6-1/2 QUARTS

LISA CLAAS WATERTOWN, WI
A batch of this colorful, crunchy snack mix is perfect for gift giving or serving at a holiday party.

4 quarts plain popped popcorn

5 cups miniature pretzels

2 cups packed brown sugar

1 cup butter, cubed

1/2 cup dark corn syrup

1/2 teaspoon salt

1/2 teaspoon baking soda

1 cup salted peanuts

2 cups non-chocolate candy (gumdrops, Skittles, etc.)

> Place popcorn and pretzels in a large bowl; set aside. In a large heavy saucepan, combine the brown sugar, butter, corn syrup and salt; cook over medium heat, stirring occasionally, until mixture comes to a rolling boil. Cook and stir until candy thermometer reads 238° (soft-ball stage). Remove from the heat; stir in baking soda. Quickly pour over popcorn and mix thoroughly; stir in peanuts.

> Turn into two greased 13-in. x 9-in. baking pans. Bake at 200° for 20 minutes; stir. Bake 25 minutes

CHARLENE CRUMP
MONTGOMERY, AL

Whenever I serve these handheld glazed cakes, they get rave reviews. Lemon and cream cheese make for a winning combination.

LEMON TEA CAKES

PREP: 30 MIN. BAKE: 10 MIN./BATCH + COOLING YIELD: 8-1/2 DOZEN

1-1/2 cups butter, softened

1 package (8 ounces) cream cheese, softened

2-1/4 cups sugar

6 eggs

3 tablespoons lemon juice

2 teaspoons lemon extract

1 teaspoon vanilla extract

1-1/2 teaspoons grated lemon peel

3 cups all-purpose flour

GLAZE:

5-1/4 cups confectioners' sugar

1/2 cup plus 3 tablespoons milk

3-1/2 teaspoons lemon extract

> In a large bowl, cream the butter, cream cheese and sugar until light and fluffy. Add eggs, one at a time, beating well after each addition. Beat in the lemon juice, extracts and lemon peel. Add flour; beat just until moistened.

> Fill greased miniature muffin cups two-thirds full. Bake at 325° for 10-15 minutes or until a toothpick comes out clean. Cool for 5 minutes before removing from pans to wire racks to cool completely.

> In a small bowl, combine the glaze ingredients. Dip the tops of cakes into glaze; place on waxed paper to dry.

tips&ideas

A lot of appetizers, such as Lemon Tea Cakes, are baked in miniature muffin tins. A curved grapefruit knife is the perfect tool for popping the bite-sized gems out of the mini muffin tins.

CATHY WALERIUS
MOUND, MN

Bite-size treats are a nice addition to a dessert buffet. Store cooled, baked tart shells in an airtight container at room temperature overnight or in the freezer for a few weeks.

CHEESE-FILLED SHORTBREAD TARTLETS

PREP: 25 MIN. + CHILLING BAKE: 20 MIN./BATCH + COOLING YIELD: 3 DOZEN

1 package (8 ounces) cream cheese, softened

1 cup sweetened condensed milk

1/3 cup lemon juice

1 teaspoon vanilla extract

1 cup butter, softened

1-1/2 cups all-purpose flour

1/2 cup confectioners' sugar

1 tablespoon cornstarch

Fresh raspberries, kiwi and mint sprigs, optional

> In a small bowl, beat cream cheese until smooth. Gradually beat in milk, lemon juice and vanilla. Cover and refrigerate for 8 hours or overnight.

> In another small bowl, beat the butter, flour, confectioners' sugar and cornstarch until smooth. Roll into 1-in. balls. Place in greased miniature tart pans or muffin cups; press onto the bottom and up the sides. Prick with a fork.

> Bake at 325° for 20-25 minutes or until golden brown. Immediately run a knife around each tart to loosen completely. Cool in pans on wire racks.

> Pipe or spoon 1 tablespoon cream cheese filling into each tart shell. Cover and refrigerate until set. Just before serving, garnish with raspberries, kiwi and mint if desired.

PEANUT BUTTER
MINI MUFFINS

PREP/TOTAL TIME: 25 MIN. YIELD: 4 DOZEN

CONNIE BARZ SAN ANTONIO, TX

These miniature muffins are just as perfect as a dessert option as they are packed in kids' lunches. The versatile mix also makes regular-size muffins for when big batches are needed.

1-3/4 cups all-purpose flour

2/3 cup packed brown sugar

2-1/2 teaspoons baking powder

1/4 teaspoon salt

1 egg

3/4 cup milk

2/3 cup chunky peanut butter

1/4 cup canola oil

1-1/2 teaspoons vanilla extract

2/3 cup miniature semisweet chocolate chips

> In a large bowl, combine the flour, brown sugar, baking powder and salt. In another bowl, combine the egg, milk, peanut butter, oil and vanilla. Stir into dry ingredients just until moistened. Fold in chocolate chips.

> Fill greased or paper-lined miniature muffin cups two-thirds full. Bake at 350° for 15-17 minutes or until a toothpick comes out clean. Cool for 5 minutes before removing from pans to wire racks.

Editor's Note: Twelve regular-size muffin cups may be used; bake for 22-25 minutes.

Editor's Note: Reduced-fat or generic brands of peanut butter are not recommended for this recipe.

WHITE CHOCOLATE
PRETZEL SNACK

PREP/TOTAL TIME: 20 MIN. YIELD: 1 DOZEN

ESTELLE CUMMINGS CAMBRIDGE, MD

I often make these sweet, crunchy clusters during the holidays. They are nice to have on hand to serve company or to take as a hostess gift. This snack is extremely easy to make, and is a great way to get kids involved in the kitchen.

1/2 cup pretzel sticks

1/2 cup salted peanuts

1/2 cup crisp rice cereal

4 squares (1 ounce each) white baking chocolate

1 teaspoon shortening

> In a large bowl, combine the pretzels, peanuts and cereal. In a microwave, melt chocolate and shortening, stir until smooth.

> Pour over pretzel mixture; toss to coat evenly. Drop mixture by heaping tablespoonfuls onto waxed paper; cool.

strawberries and pineapple over cream cheese layer; sprinkle with pecans.

> In a small microwave-safe bowl, melt chocolate and butter; stir until smooth. Drizzle over fruit. Cover and refrigerate for 1 hour.

STRIPED CHOCOLATE POPCORN SNACK

PREP: 15 MIN. + STANDING YIELD: 17 CUPS

MARY SCHMITTINGER COLGATE, WI

For a bake sale last year, I wanted to try something different. I discovered chocolate popcorn in a candy shop once and thought I'd experiment making it at home. This decadent creation was an absolute success.

12 cups popped popcorn

2 cups miniature pretzels

1 cup pecan halves, toasted

1/4 cup butter, melted

4 ounces white candy coating, coarsely chopped

2 ounces milk chocolate candy coating, coarsely chopped

> In a large bowl, combine the popcorn, pretzels and pecans. Drizzle with butter and toss; set aside.

> In a microwave, melt white candy coating at 70% power for 1 minute; stir. Microwave at additional 10- to 20-second intervals, stirring until smooth. Drizzle over popcorn mixture; toss to coat. Spread on foil-lined baking sheets.

> In a microwave, melt milk chocolate coating; stir until smooth. Drizzle over popcorn mixture. Let stand in a cool place until chocolate is set. Store in an airtight container.

Editor's Note: This recipe was tested in a 1,100-watt microwave.

FRUITY BROWNIE PIZZA

PREP: 20 MIN. + CHILLING BAKE: 15 MIN. + COOLING
YIELD: 12-14 SERVINGS

NANCY JOHNSON LAVERNE, OK

I start with a basic brownie mix to create the crust for this luscious treat that's sure to impress company. Sometimes I add mandarin oranges for even more color and flavor.

1 package fudge brownie mix (8-inch square pan size)

1 package (8 ounces) cream cheese, softened

1/3 cup sugar

1 can (8 ounces) pineapple tidbits

1 small firm banana, sliced

1 medium kiwifruit, peeled and sliced

1 cup sliced fresh strawberries

1/4 cup chopped pecans

1 square (1 ounce) semisweet chocolate

1 tablespoon butter

> Prepare brownie batter according to package directions. Spread onto a greased 12-in. pizza pan. Bake at 375° for 15-20 minutes or until a toothpick inserted near the center comes out clean. Cool completely.

> In a large bowl, beat cream cheese and sugar until smooth. Spread over brownie crust. Drain pineapple, reserving juice. Toss banana slices with juice; drain well. Arrange the banana, kiwi,

tips&ideas

Get creative with serving containers for sweet snacks such as Striped Chocolate Popcorn. Scoop individual servings into unused Chinese take-out boxes or create festive cones with pretty pieces of decorative scrapbooking paper. Guests will love the extra-special touch.

KARIN POROSLAY
WESLEY CHAPEL, FL

These plump berries filled with a creamy pudding mixture are an eye-fetching contribution to parties or special events.

CREAM-FILLED STRAWBERRIES

PREP: 30 MIN. + CHILLING   YIELD: 18 STRAWBERRIES

18 large fresh strawberries

1 cup cold fat-free milk

1 package (1 ounce) sugar-free instant vanilla pudding mix

2 cups reduced-fat whipped topping

1/4 teaspoon almond extract

> Remove stems from strawberries; cut a deep X in the top of each berry. Spread berries apart.

> In a bowl, whisk milk and pudding mix for 2 minutes. Fold in whipped topping and almond extract. Pipe or spoon about 5 teaspoons into each berry. Chill until serving.

tips&ideas

Garnish a tray of Cream-Filled Strawberries with a few strawberry fans. To do this, place a firm ripe berry with the stem down on a cutting board. With a sharp knife, make cuts, 1/8 in. apart through the berry to within 1/8 in. of the stem. Use your fingers to gently spread apart the slices to form a fan.

general index

HOT APPETIZERS (Continued)

Ham Asparagus Spirals, 32
Hearty Poppers, 51
Honey Garlic Ribs, 54
Hot & Spicy Cranberry Dip, 13
Hot Wings, 47
Jalapeno Chicken Wraps, 43
Orange-Glazed Smokies, 56
Peppered Chicken Pizza, 78
Mini Burgers with the Works, 74
Mini Hot Dogs 'n' Meatballs, 51
Mini Sausage Bundles, 37
Mini Spinach Frittatas, 77
Mozzarella Tomato Tartlets, 74
Nutty Stuffed Mushrooms, 55
Pepper-Crusted Tenderloin
   Crostini, 82
Prosciutto-Wrapped Apricots, 55
Ranch Pizza Pinwheels, 40
Raspberry Fondue Dip, 15
Reuben Spread, 17
Roasted Goat Cheese with Garlic, 12
Roasted Pepper Tart, 84
Stuffed Butterflied Shrimp, 57
Tortellini with Roasted Red
   Pepper Dip, 9
Turkey Egg Rolls, 35
Veggie Shrimp Egg Rolls, 36

KABOBS & SKEWERS

Antipasto Kabobs, 71
Appetizer Chicken Kabobs, 46
Chicken Satay, 56
Fruit and Cheese Kabobs, 67
Grilled Pork Skewers, 48
Marinated Sausage Kabobs, 65
Tortellini Appetizers, 60

NUTS

Asian Spring Rolls, 39
Baklava Tartlets, 102
Barbecued Peanuts, 24
Chicken Satay, 56
Cranberry Camembert Pizza, 80
Curried Pecans, 25
Deluxe Caramel Corn, 102
Fruit and Caramel Brie, 9
Ham Cream Cheese Balls, 67
Holiday Almonds, 21
Nutty Stuffed Mushrooms, 55

Party Cheese Balls, 10
Pesto Chili Peanuts, 22
Roasted Peanut Salsa, 7
Spicy Cashews, 28
Spicy Pecans 'n' Cranberries, 26
Striped Chocolate Popcorn
   Snack, 106
Sugar 'n' Spice Nuts, 21
White Chocolate Pretzel Snack, 105

PASTA

Antipasto Kabobs, 71
Breaded Ravioli, 52
Tortellini Appetizers, 60
Tortellini with Roasted Red
   Pepper Dip, 9

PORK, HAM & SAUSAGE

(also see bacon)

Antipasto Kabobs, 71
Appetizer Meatballs, 48
Aussie Sausage Rolls, 40
Black Forest Ham Pinwheels, 38
Cajun Canapes, 75
Crab 'n' Brie Strudel Slices, 41
Glazed Kielbasa, 47
Grilled Pork Skewers, 48
Ham 'n' Cheese Biscuit Stacks, 85
Ham Asparagus Spirals, 32
Ham Cream Cheese Balls, 67
Honey Garlic Ribs, 54
Hot & Spicy Cranberry Dip, 13
Marinated Sausage Kabobs, 65
Mini Hot Dogs 'n' Meatballs, 51
Mini Spinach Frittatas, 77
Orange-Glazed Smokies, 56
Party Pitas, 76
Prosciutto-Wrapped Apricots, 55
Ranch Pizza Pinwheels, 40

ROLL-UPS,
WRAPS & SANDWICHES

Asian Spring Rolls, 39
Aussie Sausage Rolls, 40
Black Forest Ham Pinwheels, 38
Cheesy Onion Roll-Ups, 33
Chicken Lettuce Wraps, 42
Chicken Turnovers, 35
Chicken Wonton Rolls, 32
Crab 'n' Brie Strudel Slices, 41

Cranberry Feta Pinwheels, 39
Crispy Caribbean Veggie
   Wraps, 34
Cucumber Party Sandwiches, 69
Ham 'n' Cheese Biscuit Stacks, 85
Ham Asparagus Spirals, 32
Jalapeno Chicken Wraps, 43
Mini Burgers with the Works, 74
Mini Sausage Bundles, 37
Party Pitas, 76
Ranch Pizza Pinwheels, 40
Ranch Tortilla Roll-Ups, 36
Turkey Egg Rolls, 35
Turkey Tortilla Spirals, 43
Veggie Shrimp Egg Rolls, 36

SALSA

Chunky Bloody Mary Salsa, 6
Cran-Apple Salsa, 17
Fruit Salsa with Cinnamon Chips, 10
Roasted Peanut Salsa, 7

SEAFOOD

Coconut Shrimp with Dipping
   Sauce, 53
Crab 'n' Brie Strudel Slices, 41
Crab-Stuffed Cones, 62
Grits 'n' Shrimp Tarts, 83
Shrimp Salad on Endive, 64
Smoked Salmon Cherry
   Tomatoes, 68
Stuffed Butterflied Shrimp, 57
Veggie Shrimp Egg Rolls, 36
Zesty Marinated Shrimp, 68

SNACK MIXES & MUNCHIES

Barbecued Peanuts, 24
Buttery Tortilla Snack Strips, 29
Curried Pecans, 25
Deluxe Caramel Corn, 102
Fiery Potato Chips, 23
Flavored Oyster Crackers, 25
Holiday Almonds, 21
Hot Mustard Popcorn, 22
Orange-Cranberry Snack Mix, 22
Parmesan Party Mix, 29
Parmesan Pretzel Rods, 20
Pesto Chili Peanuts, 22
Pizza Popcorn, 27
Spicy Cashews, 28

alphabetical index